PRACTICAL GUIDE TO POTTERY

PRACTICAL GUIDE TO POTTERY

Colin Gerard

BARRON'S
Woodbury, New York

First published in 1977 by
William Luscombe Publisher Limited
The Mitchell Beazley Group
Artists House
14–15 Manette Street
London W1V 5LB

© by Colin Gerard 1977

All Rights Reserved. No part of this
publication may be reproduced, stored
in a retrieval system, or transmitted,
in any form, or by any means,
electronic, mechanical, photocopying,
recording or otherwise, without the
prior permission of the Copyright owner.

ISBN 0–8120–5187–4

Library of Congress
Catalog Number 77–80602

First U.S. Edition 1977

Barron's Educational Series, Inc.
113 Crossways Park Drive
Woodbury, New York 11797

Printed in GREAT BRITAIN

Reprinted 1978

CONTENTS

THE POTTER'S CRAFT

CHAPTER 1

Students and teachers of pottery face immense problems of standards and direction. Are standards of craftsmanship important? Should we leave the making of useful pots such as tableware to the industrial potter? Should we confine ourselves to exploring new ideas and making forms of novelty value?

All these questions arise because we have immense freedom of choice and we lack the security of a living cultural heritage of our own. Early industralisation has resulted in the country potter, making pots for everyday use, being a thing of the past. Instead the mass media and museums enable us to draw upon the cultures of the world. We are just as likely to be influenced by Sung Chinese, African or pre-Columban American as by our own Greek/Christian/European culture. This does not mean that there was no contact between some of the ancient cultures. There was indeed. For example, Han China was in contact with the Roman Empire and Greek amphora forms influenced Han and Tang forms.

The major difference between such influences today and in pre-industrial times is that we lack a sound foundation upon which to build and absorb outside influences. We have to choose and make decisions from the start. In addition, we lack the restriction of materials. We can choose to buy from a wide range of clays, glaze materials and equipment whereas in the past potters had to rely on materials from their own locality.

The revival of craft pottery in Britain and elsewhere owes much to Bernard Leach. When he returned to Britain from his pottery training in Japan, accompanied by Shoji Hamada, very few country potters remained and pottery was at a low ebb. By establishing his pottery in 1920 to make, above all, useful household pots at a reasonable price, and by his writings, he revived interest in pottery. His *A Potter's Book*, published in 1940, is to be recommended to all students and teachers of pottery.

It is to Bernard Leach, his students and followers throughout the world that we owe the present growth in the number of studio potters, the social acceptance of hand-made pottery and the increasing number of schools which include pottery as part of the curriculum. Unfortunately some of the work produced by studio potters is not good, particularly the souvenir-type made to exploit holiday-makers, and also that made by those who see no need to acquire at least a minimum standard of craftsmanship.

It is up to all of us to be discerning and sensitive when we buy pottery or any other craftwork, and this discernment can be greatly developed in schools by giving students the opportunity of finding out what craftsmanship is about and by helping them to recognise and appreciate beauty of form, texture and colour.

Much of the art and craft work in schools is excellent, but there is a tendency to assume that the students should be exposed to and use as many materials as is possible. When part of a general project this could well be a sound approach. For example, clay heads might be modelled and papier-mâché applied when making puppets for a play written by the students. However, the idea that crafts are merely a series of slick processes which any fool can master with a minimum of effort should be avoided, because it is dishonest, does little to help the student and does all crafts a great disservice.

I am convinced that it is better for students to study and work at one craft and so gain a genuine understanding of all that craftsmanship entails, even though there will undoubtably be insufficient time to master the craft. Michael Cardew states that it takes seven years of full-time work and study to become really proficient as a potter!

Pottery is a comparative new-comer to the school curriculum, for while a few schools introduced pottery in the 1930's it is only in the past twenty years that it has become fairly widespread. Unfortunately there have been few potters available to teach the craft, which has resulted in some schools having unused facilities, while in other schools a keen teacher with little first-hand experience of pottery has been asked to take over pottery teaching. In other schools a teacher with college training in ceramics finds teaching the subject very difficult because he is having to prepare clay and glazes, and fire kilns; all processes which might well have been done for him at college by technical assistants or lecturers.

This book is therefore intended to help teachers without a full training in pottery, or who have been misled into believing that pottery only involves making pots. Pottery involves all the processes from preparing clay to unpacking the glazed pots. It should also help the many students of pottery who attend part-time classes, including those who decide to take a set examination in the craft.

While the acquisition of skill should never be an end in itself, it is such skill that frees the potter to create the forms he desires. All students and teachers of pottery should endeavour to find the time to practise the craft and so gain a real understanding of the materials and processes used.

GLOSSARY

Every craft has its own special and specialised vocabulary, a mixture of technical terms, and words or phrases hallowed by centuries of practical use. Here then is a glossary of the main terms used by the potter. Each occurs several times in the chapters that follow, so time spent familiarising yourself with their meaning and application will certainly show dividends later as you progress through the book.

ASH Abbreviation for 'wood ash'. An ingredient of many stoneware glazes. The variety of wood and its place of growth influence the result obtained.

BAG WALL Wall of fire-brick built inside the firing chamber of gas, oil, wood and coal-burning kilns to deflect the flames upwards. This assists in obtaining a firing of even temperature.

BALL CLAY Whitest of the secondary or sedimentary clays. Ball clays are very plastic and form the basis of most made-up clay bodies.

BANDING WHEEL Circular, free-spinning turntable. Used when decorating and when building coil pots.

BATTS Wooden boards or asbestos sheeting upon which finished pots are placed. Circular batts are used on the wheel-head when throwing large pots, or for pots which would otherwise be difficult to lift off the wheel.

BISCUIT (BISQUE) Unglazed ware which has been fired. It is usually porous, most biscuit firings being between 980°C and 1,000°C. Industrial potteries sometimes use high biscuit firings.

BLOATING Bubbles of various sizes which develop in the clay of a pot during glaze firing. An unpleasant clay/firing fault.

BODY A clay mixture of various clays and other materials such as felspar, quartz and sand. Most clays used by potters are clay bodies. Clays are not usually suitable for use in the form in which they are dug out of the ground.

BUFF CLAY Clays which fire to a cream, light tan colour.

BUNG Stopper used to fill the spy-hole of a kiln. Usually a cone-shaped piece of fire-brick.

BURNISHING The polishing of a leather-hard pot to give a smooth, semi-shiny surface.

CALCINE The heating of a material to change it physically or chemically. For example, flint pebbles are broken up by heating and clays to be used in glazes are sometimes calcined to make them less plastic.

CALLIPERS Compasses with curved lips for measuring the diameter of pots and lids.

CARBORUNDUM STONE Hand-grinding stone used to clean the bottom of glaze-fired pots, making them smooth.

CARBORUNDUM POWDER Silicon carbide which, when mixed 50/50 with China clay and sufficient water to make a paste, is used to grind-in lids, so giving a smooth, non-grating fit.

CELADON Name used to describe a range of stoneware and porcelain glazes obtained by using small quantities (0.5–3%) of iron oxide in a clear glaze, fired in reducing conditions. Colour varies from grey/blue to deep green.

CENTRING The process of getting the clay in the middle of the potter's wheel before the pot is opened out and thrown.

CERAMIC Word derived from the Greek *keramos*, meaning 'burnt stuff'. Now used to describe any process using silica and heat.

CHATTER Corrugations that can develop on the surface of a pot when it is being turned.

CHINA CLAY Almost pure clay

GLOSSARY

($Al_2O_2SiO_2 2H_2O$). It is a primary clay, white in colour and non-plastic. Used for making up white clay bodies such as porcelain, and as a glaze ingredient. It is sometimes known as 'kaolin', a word of Chinese derivation.

CHUCK   A ring or cup of clay used to support a pot while turning the base.

CHÜN GLAZES   Glazes developed in China which are opalescent blue in colour.

COILING   A method of building pots from coils or 'sausages' of clay. An ancient technique still in use today and an excellent method to use in schools.

COLLARING   The process of reducing the diameter of the neck of a pot on the wheel.

CONE   Pyrometric cones are placed in the kiln so that they are visible through the spy-hole. They are made of glaze material and are stamped with a reference number indicating the temperatures at which they will bend. By observing the cones (usually three) through the spy-hole, an accurate indication of when firing is complete can be obtained.

CONING   Movement used to centre the clay on the wheel prior to throwing. Sometimes known as 'balling and coning'.

CORNISH STONE   An English felspar found in Cornwall in the extreme south-west of the Island. Used in earthenware and stoneware glazes, and in clay bodies.

CRACKLE   Means the same as 'crazing' (q.v.), but the term 'crackle' is used when the effect is required and intentioned. Fine cracks develop in the glaze, rather like crazy paving. On porcelain it can be very pleasant and decorative. Was much used on Chinese pots.

CRANK MIXTURE   A heavily grogged (q.v.) clay used for making kiln furniture. Very useful when making large hand-built pots and sculptures.

CRAWLING   A glaze fault, but sometimes used to obtain a decorative effect. The glaze moves during firing to give islands of thick glaze with unglazed areas in between.

CRAZING   The development of fine cracks in the glaze due to the latter contracting more than the clay body, when the pot cools after firing. In earthenware this results in the pot being porous. See *Crackle*

CUTTING OFF   Passing a fine wire of twisted strands, or a nylon line, under a pot to separate it from the wheel-head or the batt upon which it has been made.

DEFLOCCULATION   The addition of a material that will assist in keeping particles in suspension in water. For example, glazes containing very little clay will tend to settle into a hard mass at the bottom of the bucket. The addition of

1–2% of Bentonite will reduce this tendency and keep the particles in suspension. Bentonite is therefore a deflocculant.

DUNTING   The cracking of pots in the kiln due to uneven cooling and draughts. Large pots are more prone to dunting.

EARTHENWARE   Pots which have a porous body and require glaze to make them water-tight. Such pots are usually fired up to 1,100°C, although some are fired to to 1,200°C. The clay colour varies from the white used in the commercial pottery industry to the red/brown wares of the country potters. Most industrially-made pots are earthenwares.

ENAMEL   Enamel colours are pigments mixed with a low firing glaze (690°–800°C). They are applied to already-fired glazed pots, to obtain bright decorative effects.

ENGOBE   American term for *slip* (q.v.), but frequently applied to slips that vitrify and so become like a glaze.

EUTECTIC   That mixture of two or more materials that gives the lowest melting point. Most stoneware materials have very high melting points, and it is only the fact that when combined in given amounts they meet at a lower temperature that allows us to use them in glazes.

FEATHERING   A decorative technique in which slip-trailed lines and dots are drawn out with a thin pliable tool, such as the sharpened end of a feather. The trailed lines must be applied to a wet slip background. This method of decoration was much used in the earthenware dishes and platter made by country potters up to the early 20th century.

FELSPAR (FELDSPAR)   Potash Felspar and Soda Felspar are common stoneware glaze ingredients.

FIRE CLAY   A sedimentary clay, usually found near coal seams and used for making bricks that will withstand high temperature. It is used by some potters when making clay bodies.

FIRING   The heating or baking of clay, usually in a kiln, to change it into pottery. The process is irreversible and a minimum temperature of 600°C is required.

FLUTING   The cutting of grooves into the leather-hard surface of a pot. A bamboo tool is usually used and the technique has been employed since the Chinese T'ang dynasty.

FLUX   Material used in glazes to assist and lower the melting point of the other glaze material. There are many such materials, common ones being Whiting (CaO), Potash (K_2O), Boric Oxide (B_2O_3) and Lead Oxide (PbO).

FOOT RING   Many pots, particularly bowls, are improved if they spring up

from a foot ring. It is usually formed when turning the leather-hard pot, but it can be thrown onto the base of the pot.

FORMULA   Chemical description, in notation form, of a material or group of materials.

FRIT   Glass-like non-soluble material which is combined with other soluble materials (e.g. borax), and ground up into a powder ready for use in a glaze. Prepared glazes sold by potters' merchants are usually fritted so as to ensure an even mix.

GLAZE   A glass-like material, differing from window glass and glassware in that it contains alumina which makes it remain viscous (sticky). As a result it remains on the pot instead of running off, and provides a smooth 'glazed' surface.

GROG   Fired biscuit (q.v.) ware that is ground up and added to clay bodies to give texture, reduce shrinkage during drying and also provide 'bite' when throwing large pots. Grog ranges from fine powder to large chunks of up to 1 cm ($\frac{3}{8}$ in) in diameter.

HAKEME   Ancient technique in which thick white slip is applied with a coarse brush.

INLAY   Decorative technique where clay is inlaid with clay of another colour.

KAOLIN   See *China Clay*

KAOLINITE   The mineralogical name for 'ideal' clay. Such clay does not in fact exist, China clay approaching most nearly to it.

KILN   The oven in which pots are fired.

KILN FURNITURE   Shelves and props used to support pots during firing.

KNEADING   Means of mixing clay of uneven consistency or colour and of removing air bubbles. Also known as 'spiral kneading', and is similar in action to kneading bread dough.

LEAD GLAZES   Due to the concern about possible health risks, it is better for schools not to use lead glazes. However, if lead frits are used in a *reliable and proven* recipe and *fired to the specified temperatures*, they should be safe.

LEATHER-HARD   A stage during the drying of clay when it has become rigid but not dry. Another description for the same stage is 'cheese-hard'. It is at this stage that thrown pots are turned, hand-built pots scraped and burnished, cut and fluted decoration carried out, and slip decoration applied.

LEVIGATION   The separation of fine and coarser particles of clay by flowing a stream of slip through a channel which has special dams across it. The fine particles flow over the dams, while the coarser particles sink to the bottom and are trapped.

LUSTRE   Metallic decoration applied to an already glazed ware. Silver, copper and gold coloured lustres are the most common.

MAJOLICA   Painting with metal oxides onto a white tin earthenware glaze.

MATT   A non-shiny surface.

MOULD   Any form over which, or into which, clay can be placed to produce a special shape. Most clay moulds are made of biscuit-fired clay or plaster of Paris.

OPACITY   When light cannot pass through a glaze.

OXIDISED FIRING   Pots fired in a clear atmosphere with plenty of air. Electric kilns normally have an oxidised atmosphere and gas, oil and wood-firing kilns can give an oxidised atmosphere if carefully controlled to do so.

PINCH POTS   Also known as *thumb pots*. Small simple pots made by pressing the thumb into a ball of clay and squeezing the clay between the thumb and fingers into a hollow shape. This method has been used since early times.

PITCHER   A large jug.

PLASTICITY   Property of clay which allows it to be altered in shape and thickness, and to maintain the new shape. It is this property that permits clay to be formed into pots and various other forms.

PORCELAIN   A white-firing stoneware clay first used in China in the T'ang dynasty. Westerners expect it to be white, vitrified, translucent and resonant.

PROP   Refractory kiln furniture used to support kiln shelves. They are made in various sizes and shapes, cylinders of about 35 mm (1⅜ in) being the most common.

PUG MILL   Machine used to mix clay of uneven consistency into a smooth consolidated mass. It consists of either a vertical or a horizontal tapered cylinder through which rotates a shaft of angled blades. A useful piece of equipment in a busy pottery.

PYROMETER   Instrument for measuring high temperature. Kilns are frequently fitted with such an instrument, which sometimes forms part of an automatic firing device.

RAKU   Low temperature earthenware, evolving from Japanese tea-ceremony pots. The pots are placed into a pre-heated kiln and removed from the red hot kiln with the aid of tongs.

RED CLAY   A secondary clay found in many areas. The colour is due to the presence of iron, and such clays are normally very plastic.

REDUCTION   During a glaze firing, the amount of oxygen in the firing chamber is reduced. This causes glazes containing iron and copper to change colour. For example, celadon glazes require a reduction firing.

REFRACTORIES   Materials used in a kiln, all of which must withstand high temperatures without deforming or breaking. Such materials are kiln shelves, bricks, shelf props and saggars (q.v.).

ROULETTE   An incised cylinder or wheel used to impress decoration into wet or damp clay.

SAGGAR   Clay box into which pots are placed prior to glaze-firing to protect them from direct flame and ash deposits.

SALT GLAZE   Type of stoneware resulting from common salt being thrown into the fire-mouth of the kiln. The salt combines with the silica in the clay, so forming a glaze.

SAWDUST FIRING   Simple method of firing, whereby pots are placed in sawdust, and the latter is allowed to smoulder.

SGRAFFITO   Method of decorating by scratching through slip, colour wash or glaze.

SHATTERING   Fault in glaze and clay body, where the glaze compresses the clay, causing the pot to break.

SHIVERING   Fault similar to shattering, except that the glaze breaks away from the clay instead of breaking the pot.

SHORT CLAY   Clay lacking in plasticity and therefore difficult to form.

SINTERING   Stage in firing clay when particles start to fuse together. This usually happens at about 800°C but the temperatures vary with different clays.

SLAB POTS   Pots made by joining or binding slabs of clay.

SLIP   Liquid clay that has been stirred to a smooth consistency. It is used to decorate by dipping, trailing, feathering, wax-resist, sgraffito, hakeme etc. Slips can be coloured by adding colouring oxides.

SLIP CASTING   Method of making pots, whereby slip is poured into plaster moulds so as to leave a thin wall of clay. This is basically an industrial method, and is not therefore dealt with in this book.

SLIP TRAILER   Usually a stiff rubber bulb with a fine nozzle, used to trail a line of slip. Rather like using an icing bag in cake-making.

SLURRY   Slushy, wet clay that can be used for joining clay to clay.

SOLUBLE   Those materials which will dissolve in a liquid. They are not used in pottery making, except when made insoluble by fritting (q.v.).

SOURING   Leaving clay for a period before using, so as to improve its plasticity.

SPONGE   A small natural sponge is essential equipment for the potter, particularly when throwing on the wheel.

STILT   A small, three-armed and pointed piece of kiln furniture, upon which earthenware glazed pots are stood for firing.

STONEWARE   High fired ware, having a glaze firing range of approx. 1,200–1,300°C. The clay is usually non-porous or nearly so, without a glaze. Developed in Han and T'ang China, and now much favoured by studio potters.

TENMUKU   Group of stoneware glazes containing upwards of 4% iron oxide, and varying in colour from red/brown to black.

TEMPLATE   Sheet of paper, card, wood or metal cut to a given shape and used as a pattern when cutting out pieces of clay.

TERRACOTTA   Unglazed red earthenware, sometimes coarse in texture.

THROWING   Process of making a pot by hand, using a revolving potter's wheel.

TRAILING   Decorative technique where slip or glaze is extruded through a nozzle onto a pot.

TRANSLUCENT   Permitting light to pass through, but not transparent. Thin porcelain is translucent.

TRANSPARENT   Transmitting light without obstruction. Clear glass is an obvious example.

TURNING   Trimming of a pot on the wheel, usually its base. The clay is normally leather-hard and a sharp metal tool is used.

TURNING TOOLS   Tools, normally metal, used for turning leather-hard pots.

UNDERGLAZE COLOURS   Pigments applied to an unfired or biscuited pot before the application of glaze. Metal oxides or specially fritted colours can be used, and they are usually mixed with clay and water.

VITREOUS   Glassy. Fired to a high enough temperature, clay will vitrify, but there is a danger of it being deformed. Stoneware is partly vitrified, and porcelain completely so.

WARPING   The deforming of a pot at any stage of its manufacture.

WAX   Either a heated mixture of paraffin wax and thin lubricating oil, or a proprietary wax emulsion. Used as a resist for both slips and glazes. It is a useful decorative technique and an aid when glazing pots.

WEDGING   A means of mixing clays of different consistency and/or colour; also of removing air bubbles prior to using the clay.

WHITING   Potter's name for calcium carbonate (chalk/lime). A useful flux in stoneware glazes.

BASIC
MATERIALS

Plate 1. Out of the ground! The Trethosa China Clay pit, near St. Austell, Cornwall, in Britain's South West.

Geological background

Clay has been, and continues to be, formed by the geologic weathering of the earth's crust. This is a continuous process, goes on everywhere, and therefore clay is common and generally abundant.

It is difficult for us to realise that geological changes are taking place at all times, for we can only observe the earth for the relatively short period of our lives.

In remote geological time the earth was a molten mass. The relatively thin surface or crust (30 km) froze, covering a very hot interior. Before the surface froze, heavier material—such as metals —tended to sink to the centre, leaving the crust of fairly uniform composition. Rocks formed during this cooling are called *igneous* rocks.

The variety of rocks and minerals we associate with the earth is largely the result of later changes. Below a depth of about 1,000 m the rock is mainly basalt.

As the earth cooled various minerals were formed by varying conditions, such as slight differences in the composition of the molten material, different pressures, and different rates of cooling. However the small number of minerals formed is illustrated by the following list giving the approximate percentages of the various minerals making up the earth's crust:

Felspar	59.5
Ferro-magnesian group	16.8
Quartz	12.0
Biotite	3.8
Titanium minerals	1.5
All others	6.4
	100.0

Felspar, the most common mineral, when weathered accounts for most clay. Many other minerals have been identified but most are rare.

Since the formation of the earth's crust geological changes have occurred. Water has been responsible for many of these changes. Over millions of years it has dissolved soluble matter from rocks, so making the oceans salt, and it has gradually ground rock on rock, so breaking them into ever smaller pieces.

Another cause of change has been the injection of gases and heat from below the earth's crust. This sometimes results in volcanos, but hot gases are still released in many parts of the world—such as New Zealand—without molten matter being deposited.

The Formation of Clay

Primary Clay

China Clay (Kaolin)

At one time it was thought that clay was formed by the deep weathering of granite into felspar and then into kaolin. However, geologists now agree that it was formed in three stages by chemical action from below the granite; this is known as pneumatolysis. This chemical action, thought to have taken place 280 million years ago, consisted of the injection of gases at high pressure and temperature (perhaps 400°C). The first stage turned some of the minerals to tourmaline; this tourmaline was unaffected by the second and third stages and it can be found in large lumps.

The second stage involved fluorine vapours attacking the granite, so forming, among others, topaz and fluorspar, the latter being found in 'Cornish Stone', a common stoneware glaze ingredient.

The third stage involved the injection of the gases CO_2 (carbon dioxide) and H_2O (water vapour). This did not affect the quartz or tourmaline but converted the felspar (50%–60% of whole rock) into kaolin and a form of mica.

Kaolin is said to have the molecular formula Al_2O_3 $2SiO_2$ $2H_2O$. That is, one molecule of Al_2O_3 (Alumina) is associated with two molecules of SiO_2 (silica) and two molecules of H_2O (water). It should be noted that this is a theoretical formula and is not found in nature without additional oxides.

Extraction of Kaolin

Kaolin is extracted on an industrial scale by playing a powerful jet of water on the rock face, so washing out the clay and mica from the course quartz and tourmaline grains. The mica is then separated from the clay by a system of running the milky suspension of clay and mica down troughs with 'riffles' to catch the mica particles. The clay is then dried and pulverised. The 'White

BASIC MATERIALS

Mountains' near St. Austell in Cornwall are really heaps of the unwanted quartz, not clay. Most British china clay is found in Cornwall.

China clay (kaolin) is known as 'Primary Clay' because it is formed on the site of the parent rock and is not a sedimentary rock.

Secondary clay—Sedimentary

As with china clay, secondary clays are for the most part derived from an igneous rock, usually a member of the felspar family, but in some areas from volcanic deposits.

English Ball Clay

These clays are an exception among secondary clays. Their formation was somewhere between that of china clay and the sedimentary clays. They were probably formed by pneumatolysis, as was the china clay, in the Dartmoor area of the western county of Devon, but were later washed out and deposited in lake basins in South Devon, North Devon and the neighbouring county of Dorset. In addition to transporting the china clay, the water caused the particles of clay to be ground smaller and separated from the mica from the clay. Hence the resulting clays are remarkably pure and due to the small particle size, very plastic. The Dorset clays had to travel further and as a result are less pure than the Devon clays. Some of the variation in colour is caused by carbonaceous matter (plant growth) which burns out during firing.

The origin of the name ball clay derives from the method of transporting the Devon and Dorset clays in two balls slung across a donkey's back.

Other Sedimentary Clays

Unlike china clay the rock was weathered from above by the action of water and temperature changes. As the rock was broken down the smaller particles were often removed by water and deposited elsewhere, picking up 'impurities' on the way. This removal and depositing eventually led to a clay deposit. The composition of such clays is infinitely variable due to the differing physical, geographical and geological conditions. These clays are by far the most commonly found, if not most commonly used. Glacial clays are sedimentary clays which were picked up by glaciers in the Ice Age and transported

long distances without the usual separation that water transport would have caused. Sometimes the end of a glacier would flow into the sea, break off as an iceberg and carry a large body of clay until the iceberg melted, sometimes over what is now land. This is thought to be the origin of the well-known Fremington red clay. This clay, like most glacial clays, can be dug and used as found but has a low melting point, making it only suitable for low-fired earthenware.

Another sedimentary clay is fire clay. This is found next to coal seams and was the earth in which grew the trees that became coal. The earth was later leached (percolated with water) leaving a clay high in alumina and low in fluxes, thus a refractory clay.

Bentonite

This is the most commonly used of the montmorillonite group of clays. It was formed by the weathering of volcanic ashes and lavas and its theoretical formula is

$$Al_2O_3\ 4SiO_2\ H_2O + nH_2O$$

as opposed to that of Kaolin which is:

$$Al_2O_3\ 2SiO_2\ 2H_2O$$

that is, it has twice as much silica as kaolin and has a varying additional water content. The first property makes it low firing and liable to shatter when fired. The second property, together with its very small particle size, probably less than one tenth that of kaolin, makes it very plastic and gives it a high contraction rate. This makes it unusable by itself but it is used in small quantities,

up to about 3%, to aid the plasticity of kaolin-based clays, in particular porcelain. It is also useful as a *deflocculant* in glazes: that is, it helps keep the particles in suspension and so hinders the glaze from settling in the bottom of the bin or bucket.

Plasticity of Clay

Measurement of plasticity is really very much the subjective judgement of the potter, but it can be defined as the property which permits the shape of the clay to be altered by pressure, yet retain that shape when pressure is released.

The reasons for the variation in plasticity are still inconclusive but some of the probable reasons are as follows: The clay particles are very fine. Each crystal is like a small flat sheet, which when lubricated with water, will move easily against its neighbour, while electrical attraction holds the sheets in place when pressure is released.

It has been suggested that by storing clay so that it matures, bacterial action improves the lubricating action of the water between the clay crystals. Plasticity is certainly improved if clay is allowed to mature. Clays with the greatest plasticity are not always the best in practice, for they frequently have a tendency to flop when used and often have a high shrinkage rate, which causes cracking during drying. Bentonite is an example of a highly plastic clay which cannot be used by itself but is a valuable addition to less plastic clays, such as china clay.

	Primary Clay	Secondary Clay (Sedimentary)
Formation	Rock broken down by water, steam or gas at the site of the parent rock	Transported by water, wind or glacier and broken down as it moved
Impurities	Contains few impurities. Contains no carbonaceous matter	Collected impurities such as iron, other minerals and clays. Contains carbonaceous matter, which fires out in the kiln
Plasticity	Larger particle size so non-plastic	Smaller particle size so plastic
Colour	White	Grey, buff, tan or red-brown
Examples	Kaolin or china clay	Ball clay, earthenware, fire clay

Clay Bodies

The potter is very fortunate if he has access to a clay which suits the type of ware he wishes to make without considerable modification. Country potters, who made the everyday pots for their local community, including bread crocks, kale forcers and mixing bowls, for a very low price, had of necessity to use a locally dug clay. Isaac Button of Soil Hill pottery was one such potter. He had the good fortune to have a deposit of clay which would fire in the high earthenware range and throw well without modification except for some grog for extra large pieces. Most country potters had to adapt to their clay and use it unmodified.

The necessity of adaptation is apparent when Chinese pots are studied. Most of the different wares, such as Chün and Ting derive their names from the kiln and district in which they were made. In other words, local materials and conditions tended to dictate the colour and firing temperature of the wares. The efficiency and ultimate temperature of the kiln also played a major part in deciding the type of ware to be made but the clay available was crucial. Today, labour is frequently more expensive than the raw material and potters and their customers choose a type of ware and clay for qualities other than its local availability. It is therefore necessary to mix a clay from dry clays or plastic clays plus sand or grog bought from the potter's merchant. Such mixtures are known as clay bodies. Very careful testing should be undertaken before mixing large quantities of clay so as to satisfy such requisites as plasticity, only 5–7% wet to dry shrinkage, firing range and glaze fit.

This is dealt with in greater depth in the following section.

Testing a new clay

If a very simple test is required for a sample of clay obtained from a local source, such as a building site or a sample from a new batch of mixed or delivered clay the following should be sufficient:

1. Remove any obvious impurities such as stones and plant roots. Leave for two weeks to mature.
2. Knead until of even consistency and in good condition for use.

3. Test for plasticity either by throwing a small sample, say 500 gms or try pressing a 10 mm ($\frac{1}{2}$ in) coil around a broom stick, observing if it cracks unduly. A small thumb pot is also a fair plasticity test.
4. Roll out a 10 cm (4 in) strip. Dry carefully, turning to avoid warping. Measure when dry. If contraction is over 10% the clay is unlikely to be useful as high shrinkage will cause the pots to crack when drying.
5. Biscuit fire a sample pot and a 10 cm (4 in) strip. It is best to place all tests on scrap pieces of shelf in case of disaster!
6. If the clay seems to be satisfactory after biscuit firing and a note of the shrinkage of the strip has been made the samples can be glazed and glaze fired. It is likely that an earthenware glaze and firing will prove more satisfactory.

A more thorough testing procedure is as follows:

1. Test for soluble alkalis by drying a clay sample. If a scum or white staining appears it is too high in soluble alkalis and the clay is not worth pursuing.
2. Test for lime by dropping a small piece of clay into a 50% solution of hydrochloric acid. Lime will cause bubbling. If lime is present the clay is not worth using as lime behaves like plaster of Paris, reabsorbing water after firing, expanding, and so causing lumps of clay to flake off.
3. Test for plasticity by using a well-kneaded and matured example to throw a small pot or by pressing a 10 mm ($\frac{1}{2}$ in) coil around a broom stick, observing if the clay cracks unduly.
4. Test for shrinkage by rolling out a strip about 13 cm by 4 cm and 2 cm thick. (5 × 1$\frac{1}{2}$ × $\frac{3}{4}$ in). Two marks exactly 10 cm (4 in) apart are then scored into the clay. The clay is next left to dry, turning it over as it dries to avoid warping. When it has dried, measure the distance between the scored lines. If it has shrunk to less than 9 cm (3$\frac{1}{2}$ in) the clay is not likely to be useful, as high shrinkage frequently causes pots to crack as they dry.
5. Test fire—A test strip should also be fired to biscuit and then glaze temperatures, the rate of shrinkage being noted as well as the colour, vitrification and deformation.

It is advisable to place all tests on a piece of scrap kiln shelf in case the clay

melts and ruins a good shelf.
6. If the tests have proved satisfactory the clay can be tested on the wheel for standing strength and additions of grog, sand and quartz can be tried to reduce shrinkage and alter the throwing quality of the clay.
7. Assuming that all the six tests have proved satisfactory you are very fortunate in that you have a usable clay. If it is not altogether satisfactory it could well be useful when mixed with another clay. This applies particularly to a clay which proves to have a low vitrification and deformation temperature, for it could well be used to give a high-firing clay more colour and improve its vitrification without causing deformation.

The Principal Stoneware Glaze Minerals

The stoneware potter needs very few materials in addition to clay in order to practice his craft. In fact, he could use a low melting point clay, rich in fluxes, as a glaze on top of his stoneware clay. The mud from some rivers makes a good dark Tenmuku glaze.

It is thought that the early Chinese Potters developed stoneware glazes after observing that where the ash from the kiln fire settled on their unglazed wares it formed a simple glaze. By mixing wood ash with clay and applying it all over a pot the whole pot became glazed and not just that part of the pot where the fly-ash from the kiln fire settled.

Wood ash is still a valuable glaze ingredient. It contains silica, a little alumina and fluxes. Woods vary considerably in their chemical make-up, depending on the variety of tree or plant and the type of soil in which they have grown.

The potter needs to have three basic ingredients for his stoneware glazes:

Silica A glass former—M.P. 1,160°–1,713°C.
Alumina To keep the glaze viscous and so prevent it from running off the pot—M.P. 2,050°C.
Flux To lower the melting point of the silica and alumina so that the glaze melts before the clay.

Silica

The principal sources of this essential ingredient of a glaze are from clays, wood ash, felspars, quartz and flint.

Quartz This is quite plentiful in nature both as quartz crystal and as quartz sands.

Flint This is found as pebbles, usually in chalk seams.

Flint is less pure than quartz but has the advantage of being finer grained and so more readily converts into cristobolite during firing. Flint is sometimes more difficult to buy from potters' merchants as it has to be calcined before being ground. Silica has a melting point of 1,610°–1,713°C.

Felspars

As already mentioned, felspars form the largest single group of minerals in the earth's crust—almost 60%. The formation of felspars from igneous rocks has also been mentioned in the section dealing with the formation of kaolin.

The most important members of the felspar family are:

Potash Felspar $(K_2O\ Al_2O_3\ 6SiO_2)$
Soda Felspar $(Na_2O\ Al_2O_3\ 6SiO_2)$
Lime Felspar $(CaO\ Al_2O_3\ 6SiO_2)$

All three have the same ratio of alumina to silica but they differ in that they have different principal fluxes. The formulas are theoretical, for other fluxes are usually present. For example, potash felspar has some soda present and soda felspar has some potash present.

Two other felspars are often used. One is Cornish stone, which has approximately equal quantities of the three fluxes, potash, soda and lime and some fluorspar which gives it its characteristic colours of blue/pink. It has a slightly lower melting point than the other three felspars and is often used in porcelain bodies. The other felspar is Nepheline Syenite. This has the formula:

$$Na_2O\ Al_2O_3\ 2Si\ O_2$$

It differs from the other felspars in having a relatively high alumina and lower silica content. It has a lower melting point than potash and soda felspars. Felspars melt by themselves at about 1,200°C.

So felspars do in themselves provide the essential ingredients of a stoneware glaze, namely silica, alumina and fluxes. However, they do not melt until a temperature of 1,200°C and even then the melt is sluggish and the glaze will certainly craze due to the high contraction rate of the fluxes present. Some Chinese Sung wares were glazed with a high felspathic glaze and the resultant crazed, milky, semi-opaque quality can be beautiful.

Limestone (Whiting) $CaCO_3$

This is one of the principal fluxes in stoneware glazes and ideal for lowering the melting point of a felspathic glaze. This is despite its own melting point of 2,570°C. The main source is from limestone and chalk, which are almost pure calcium $CaCO_3$. Other sources are marble and sea shells. In addition to being an excellent flux, whiting has the advantage of having a low expansion/contraction rate and is therefore useful in eliminating glaze-craze.

With the materials already mentioned a potter has all the essential ingredients for stoneware pottery. Those that follow are often desirable but not essential.

Dolomite $CaCO_3\ MgCO_3$

This mineral is found in large quantities in the Alps. It is a source of calcium and magnesium. It is very useful when making a semi-matt opaque glaze.

Talc $3MgO\ 4SiO_2\ H_2O$

This is the chief mineral found in soapstone. It provides magnesium and silica and is useful for making a glaze more viscous and less fluid, for decreasing thermal expansion and so helping to cure crazing and to give the glaze a satiny, waxy surface texture.

Barium Carbonate $BaCO_3$

An alkaline earth and the chief source of barium in a glaze. It causes the glaze surface to be dull when used in amounts of 20%+ but is valuable as a glaze base when firing stoneware in an oxidising atmosphere. Copper, as with most alkaline glazes, tends to a turquoise green as opposed to a leaf green.

It has a low expansion rate which helps in formulating a glaze that does not craze.

Bone Ash $3CaO\ P_2O_5$

This is the usual source of calcium phosphate. It is the chief ingredient of bone china but is useful in glazes as an opacifier, forming small bubbles within the glaze. It can be excellent but milkiness should be avoided.

Tin Oxide SnO_2

This is an expensive but very necessary opacifier in earthenware glazes and is also useful in stoneware. The small white tin particles remain suspended in the glaze melt instead of becoming part of the melt. Between 5% and 10% is usually added.

Lead

This is used in the form of a frit, so as to avoid the risk of poisoning associated with red, white lead, etc. The most common frits are lead-bisilicate ($PbO\ 2SiO_2$) and lead-sequisilicate ($2PbO\ 3SiO_2$).

Many earthenware glazes have a lead frit base for it gives a clear, bright glaze which colours well. It is safe if properly formulated and fired in an oxidised firing to the temperature demanded by the formula. Colouring oxides should not be used without ensuring that it is safe so to do. Copper can easily make a safe, stable glaze a hazard. Potters' suppliers have admirable pamphlets available dealing with safety and the use of lead.

Borax

Being soluble, borax is used in the form of a frit. It is often used as an alternative to or an addition to lead frit as the base of earthenware glaze. It is also added to stoneware glazes in small amounts to lower the melting point.

Plate 2. Old print showing a horse-powered clay mill in operation in the early 19th century.

PREPARATION AND STORAGE OF CLAY

Clay can be obtained in a number of ways. It can be dug locally and prepared for use; it can be mixed to a specific recipe using powdered clays and other ingredients bought from a potters' merchant; it can be bought ready-mixed from the potters' merchant either as a powder, or in a plastic state, already mixed with water.

Each method of obtaining clay—obviously the most important material the potter has to use—has advantages and disadvantages, be it of quality, cost or manual labour. Such advantages and disadvantages do not apply equally to the full-time or part-time potter. They certainly do not always apply to the teaching situation, be it in an art college, primary, secondary or high school. For example, the full-time potter will require a specific clay for his type of work; schools will generally want to offer two or more different clays so that students become aware of the variety available. The full-time potter will probably have space to install a dough-mixer with which to mix his own clay, and he will be able to devote time to using such a mixer; schools are unlikely to have the space safely to install a mixer and the teacher is unlikely to have time to use such a mixer, having to cope with a continuous stream of students and, in many cases, a subject in addition to pottery.

These are the different methods of preparing clay, their advantages and disadvantages in different situations.

Locally dug clay

Before the days of mass transportation and industrialisation most pots were made by a local potter. He was a craftsman who had to use the nearest deposit of clay available. This meant that he had to fire his pots to the temperature most suited to the clay and as most clay deposits are of secondary clay containing iron oxide, the majority of the wares produced were red earthenware fired to 1,000°–1,100°C. Luckily, such clays are usually very plastic and satisfactory for throwing.

A few potters still use locally dug clays but the number has been declining as stoneware has replaced earthenware as the preferred ware. The labour involved in digging and preparing local clay is also a handicap to its use.

It is desirable that all students are involved in preparing some local clay for use, for it makes them aware that

Plate 3. Building sites or similar excavations are possible sources for locally-dug clay, but obtain permission before investigating or digging—and then only do so under qualified supervision.

CHAPTER 3

PREPARATION AND STORAGE OF CLAY

clay really does come from the ground and that a considerable amount of labour is involved in its preparation. It is not a manufactured substance that arrives in plastic bags as if by magic!

Preparation

Seek out a deposit of clay. This is best done when deep excavations are in progress for road works, pipe laying or building. The clay will vary in colour, being anything from grey to a dark yellow/brown. It is usually firm and slimy and not crumbly like soil.

Before digging out large quantities, try a small sample for plasticity and firing temperature (see Chapter 2). This will avoid digging and carting clay for no purpose. If the small sample holds promise, a larger quantity can be dug ready for preparation.

Spread out the clay on clean bricks, board or sheeting, plaster batts or on top of a kiln. Pick out any obvious impurities—such as stones and roots—then allow the clay to become completely dry. Break the clay up until it becomes powder. One way of doing this is to crush the big pieces with a large mallet, then roll the small pieces with a rolling-pin. Depending on the quantity of clay being prepared, tip the powder into a bucket, dustbin, trash can, or tank and add water until a slurry of single cream consistency is made. Stir well, then pass the slurry through a 60-mesh sieve into another vessel.

Allow the clay to settle and then pour off the water, so leaving a thick slurry. Spread the slurry on a clean drying surface. A shallow outdoor trough is ideal but is unlikely to be available unless this is to be the usual method of clay preparation. Allow the clay to firm up evenly, turning the clay over when necessary. When firm enough to be handled the clay should be pugged, if a Pug Mill is available, or it can be wedged and kneaded. (See Chapter 4.).

The clay should then be placed in a lidded bin, or wrapped in plastic sheeting, for a few weeks so that it can mature and so become more plastic.

If the small test piece of clay proves to be very smooth and close-grained it will probably be improved by the addition of grog or sand, which will make the clay easier to use and less likely to crack when drying. Such additions can either be kneaded in by spreading the grog, etc. on the bench as the clay is kneaded, or by mixing it into the sieved slurry before the clay is left to firm-up.

Advantages and Disadvantages

The major advantages of preparing locally dug clay are its initial cheapness—it might well be free—and the fact that it demonstrates to students that clay really does come from the ground. I think students should always prepare at least a small amount of clay in this way.

The main disadvantages are the time involved in digging and preparation and the restrictions it imposes, such as the firing temperature, colour and type of ware.

Prepared Bodies

A clay body is a mixture of clays and materials like quartz, felspar and grog, that are mixed together to give a clay that will fire at a specific temperature, have a particular colour, have a known shrinkage rate and other specific qualities. A 'prepared body' is just such a clay prepared by a potters' merchant.

Plate 4. Kaolin manufacture in Cornwall, mid-19th century.

Plate 5. A pug mill can be a useful item in a school pottery.

16

Most merchants have comprehensive lists of clay, giving firing temperatures and other qualities that can be expected. They are supplied either as a dry powder (dry prepared body) or already mixed with water and pugged ready for use (plastic prepared body).

Plastic Prepared Body

Most schools prefer to buy clay in this state but the following advantages, disadvantages and considerations should be borne in mind:

Does the supplier offer a clay that is suitable for a specific use? Samples are usually available, which, together with the information available from the supplier, should answer this question.

Cost. This varies enormously for different clays and from different merchants. It is better to buy in large quantities from specialist suppliers. Buying in small quantities from Artists' suppliers can multiply the cost five-fold and more! Always allow for the cost of carriage, for plastic clay is bulky and heavy, and can add 30%–50% to the cost of the clay. A few merchants quote a price inclusive of carriage charges but this is not common and carriage charges are constantly increasing. Due to the high carriage costs it is advantageous to order an estimated year's supply at one time.

The clay is supplied in plastic bags and if kept in a shady cool place it will keep for a year or more. After delivery it should be kept for at least two weeks so that the clay can mature and become plastic. Test each new batch when delivered as potters' merchants can make errors. Such testing can prevent a kiln-full of failures!

Advantages and disadvantages: The great advantage of prepared plastic clay is that little or no preparation is necessary. The disadvantages are its relatively high cost and the limits imposed by the list of clays available, extensive though this is.

Dry Prepared Body

This method of buying a prepared body is not as popular as the plastic. Perhaps for this reason, it is not always possible to obtain the dry body, despite its being listed in suppliers' catalogues.

To prepare the clay for use it is mixed with water in a bin or tank and allowed to settle. The surplus water is syphoned off, and the resultant slurry spread on a clean board to firm up. When firm enough to handle, the clay is pugged or kneaded, and stored ready for use. An alternative to this method of preparation is to use a baker's old-fashioned dough mixer. This is discussed in the section on preparing a specific clay body. Test a sample of the batch.

Advantages and disadvantages: The only advantage of a dry prepared body over a plastic prepared body is the reduced cost of carriage, this reduction being quite considerable as local water is used instead of paying for the transport of water from the suppliers to the pottery.

The disadvantages are the limits imposed by the restricted number of bodies available and, above all, the labour involved in the mixing and preparation of the clay for use. It is almost certainly better to mix a body from basic materials, as this enables any body to be mixed and will be considerably cheaper.

Preparing a specific clay body

Most full-time potters mix their own clay bodies from basic materials such as ball-clay, fire-clay, quartz, felspar and sand. This enables them to use a clay made specifically for their types of ware, glazes and firing conditions.

The mixing of clay bodies should not be undertaken unless a number of clay trials have been satisfactorily tested. (See Chapter 10.) When a good and well-tested recipe is available larger quantities of clay can be prepared. Here are the most common methods of mixing:

Blunging

This method is used in industry and in some Art Colleges; the equipment is expensive and bulky, so unless such equipment is accessible or can be acquired secondhand it is likely to remain a text-book method of preparation.

Basically, it involves the mixing of the weighed-up clay body ingredients with water in a large tank known as a blunger. The tank contains a power-driven rotary mixer and has a large tap near the base. After thoroughly mixing the clay into a thin slurry, it is either run into shallow troughs for partial drying before pugging, or it is pumped into a filter-press—a filter-press being a large piece of equipment made up of a series of thin cast iron frames about 900 cms (3 ft) square by 5 cms (2 in), which are lined with porous filter cloths. These bags are connected to the blunger via a pump which forces the slurry into the bags. When the bags are full they are squeezed together, so removing much of the excess water in the clay. The bags are then dismantled and the clay removed for pugging.

Even if a potter or school could accommodate or afford such a piece of equipment, it is rarely suitable for stoneware bodies, as the latter contain more ultra-fine particles than earthenware or porcelain bodies and these particles are likely to block the mesh of the filter-bag, so preventing the excess water from being squeezed out.

Using a dough mixer

This method of preparing clay bodies is much favoured by studio potters and is used in some Art Colleges. If space is available in a school with a full-time pottery specialist and a technical assistant it could prove an excellent money-saving way of preparing clay.

A prerequisite is a secondhand baker's dough mixer, an increasingly precious piece of machinery as more and more potters search them out!

Using such equipment is a rather dusty and noisy business, so if it is to be used in a college or school it is essential to have it installed in a room separated from the teaching area. As more is learned of the dangers of silicosis, a lung disease caused by exposure to fine silica dust, the importance of keeping dusty processes away from people becomes even more essential. A dust mask should always be worn when using a dough mixer or, for that matter, when handling material like quartz, flint and felspar.

Method of preparation

The dry materials, except any felspar, fine quartz or flint, are tipped into the bowl of the mixer and briefly mixed. Any felspar, quartz or flint is mixed with water and sieved before being added to the dry mix. This assists in obtaining an even mix of these materials, which tend to be lumpy and difficult to distribute. Additional water is gradually

PREPARATION AND STORAGE OF CLAY

added as the clay is mixed, until the clay is of usable consistency. It is then pugged and allowed to mature before use.

Mixing by hand

Clay can be mixed from dry materials without any mechanical aids, provided the potter has the time, energy and inclination. The method is the same as for a dough mixer, except that the materials are placed in a large bin, a brick trough or on a clean floor and mixed with a shovel, gradually adding the felspar/quartz mixture and water. It is rather like mixing cement. The clay is then pugged or wedged, wrapped in plastic and matured ready for use.

A few potters mix their clay by hand in shallow troughs but add sufficient water to make it into a slurry, which is left to firm up before pugging or wedging. They claim the liquid mix gives a more thorough and even mix.

Additions of Grog or Sand

If a clay is to be used for hand-building, sculpture, tile-making or for throwing very large pots, an opening material, such as *grog* (fired and ground clay)—available in a variety of sizes from small pebbles to dust—or sand is added. This will reduce the contraction that occurs as the pot dries, and during firing, thus lessening the risk of breakage.

The size and amount of grog will vary according to the size and thickness of the pot and the texture required. A useful grog size is 30's–60's. Grog or sand can be mixed with the clay either when mixing up the day batch or by kneading it in just prior to use. The first method permits accurate weighing but the second method, which relies on the eye to judge quantities, is quite satisfactory. A disadvantage of grog is that it sometimes contains an assortment of fired clays; some of these may be unsuitable for stoneware firing and cause 'bloating'. See page 69.

Summary of the advantages and disadvantages of each method of preparation

NOTE: Always test clay before buying or mixing large quantities and ensure that it fires at the required temperature. This will avoid wasted energy and time.

Locally dug clay: An excellent project and to be recommended to all pottery students, for it gets them down to the basics of pottery, makes them understand that clay really does come from the earth and requires time and labour in preparation. It might well be free! The disadvantage of the time involved in this method will become apparent! The other disadvantage is the restriction of using the clay that the locality offers, which might be quite unsuited to individual requirements.

Plastic prepared body: Such clays have a number of advantages. Clays suitable for particular requirements can, within limits, be ordered ready for use, so cutting out the time involved in mixing and preparation.

The main disadvantage is that of cost, particularly when carriage charges are added to the cost of the clay.

Most schools find prepared plastic clay easily the most convenient for general use as the teacher usually has to undertake the preparation of clay; a dough mixer is not often available and the teacher's time is better utilized in teaching and encouraging his students than in digging or mixing clay.

Dry prepared body: The only advantage of this method of buying clay is that it is cheaper to buy than plastic clay. This advantage is far outweighed by the work involved in mixing and pugging it before use. It has not even the advantage of mixing from basic ingredients which offers a large choice of clays.

Specific clays from basic materials: Mixing a clay body from basic materials is much cheaper than buying prepared clays and gives an infinite choice of clay bodies. However, unless a dough mixer is available it is not recommended for schools due to the time and energy required in mixing. An individual potter might well find the effort involved worthwhile so as to have the clay he wants and at the cheapest price.

Storage

By whichever method clay is prepared or bought it should be stored in plastic or airtight bins, in a cool, damp place. New clay should be stored for at least two weeks, preferably three months, so as to enable the clay to 'sour' and so improve its plasticity. An unheated cellar makes an ideal clay store. Some school potteries are designed with the clay store next to the kiln! It is necessary to prepare or buy prepared bodies well before they are to be used.

Reclaiming clay

The craftsman potter has a certain amount of clay that needs reclaiming—primarily trimmings from turning. As he probably mixes his own clay he can add such trimmings to a clay batch in preparation.

The school pottery seems to amass large quantities of dry and half-dry clay which cannot be added to the next batch in preparation, as plastic clay is usually bought ready prepared. Therefore an efficient reclaiming routine needs to be established, so avoiding waste and an end-of-the-year headache!

I find it best to throw firm clay that is too dry for use, very dry pieces being broken up, and all slurry from wheels, into a large container. This container might be a cold water tank on wheels, a large metal bin or a large bin built from glazed bricks. The mixture of dry clay and slurry is mixed with a trowel or spade and left overnight so that by the morning it is ready for pugging or wedging. On occasions extra water needs to be added to the mixture.

Clay that is too wet for pugging or kneading is soon firmed up by spreading it onto absorbent boards, plaster or by making it into bridges and leaving it overnight. When the clay is removed from the board or plaster they should be cleaned and dried on a kiln or radiator. As continuous use of clay tends to reduce its plasticity, it is best to reclaim it and store it for a few days before use.

It is often better to work to some sort of system or timetable for jobs such as clay reclamation. It is not a job that can be carried out just before the clay is to be used, because the quality of the clay, in particular its plasticity, will suffer. In addition, reclaiming large quantities of clay can be a tiresome job, so it is as well to keep the amount of reclamation at any one time to a minimum. Perhaps it is also worth emphasising at this stage that the craft of pottery does not begin and end with the making of a pot or piece of sculpture, but involves the preparation of clay, kneading, making, turning, firing, glazing, glaze-firing, and last, but not least, the maintenance and cleaning of equipment. Part-time potters attending classes have a tendency to forget this.

POT-MAKING WITHOUT A WHEEL

Before a pot can be made the clay has to be chosen and then prepared. Many types of clay and their properties have been discussed in the preceding chapter, but in practice one's choice may be limited by circumstances. However, different clays are recommended for each type of pot in case a choice is available. Much depends on the size and scope of the pottery in which one is working, and the firing temperature of the kiln and the clay.

Clay preparation

It is essential that clays of all types are properly and thoroughly prepared before use. Preparation is sometimes laborious and frequently time consuming but it is only fools who think that they can make satisfactory pots without having the clay in good condition.

To be in good condition the clay must satisfy the following:

1. It must be well matured so that it is plastic.

2. It must have the correct water content. That is, it must not be too wet or too dry for its proposed use. If it is too wet it can be kneaded, on an absorbent board or a block of plaster. This will soon firm-up clay that is a little too wet. However, if the clay is much too wet it can either be spread out on an absorbent board or on plaster and left for an hour or so before kneading. Alternatively it can be made into a series of arches (Fig. 1A), and left in a well-aired place until the clay becomes suitably firm. The clay is then kneaded before use.

It is worth noting that clay, including newly-made pots, dries more evenly when exposed to moving air, such as in a breeze outdoors, than when subjected to heat, such as the top of a hot kiln.

If the clay is too firm but not so dry that it warrants reclaiming, the quickest way to soften it is to make a block of the clay and cut it with a wire into slices about 10 mm ($\frac{1}{2}$ in) thick. The slices can either (a) be placed into a bowl of water for about ten minutes or (b) the fingers can be pressed into a slice so making small indentations, water splashed into these indentations, another slice placed on the wet slice and the procedure repeated until the block is reassembled. After allowing the water to soak into the clay it should be well-kneaded. Some

CHAPTER 4

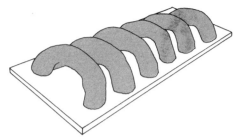

Fig. 1A. Drying clay. Clay too wet to use can be placed on a board in a series of arches until it is firm enough to knead.

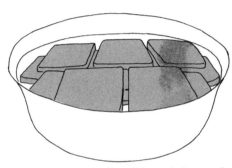

Fig. 1B. Softening clay. Slices of clay can be left to soak in a bowl of water before wedging and kneading.

Fig. 1C. Another method of softening clay. Indentations are made in slices of clay with the fingers, and the clay is then splashed with water.

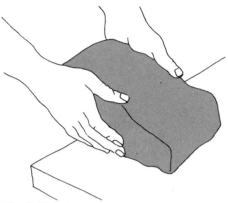

Fig. 2. Wedging
2A: The block of clay is slammed down onto the bench so that it projects over the edge. *Stage 1*

2B: The clay is cut in half by an upward movement of the cutting wire. *Stage 2*

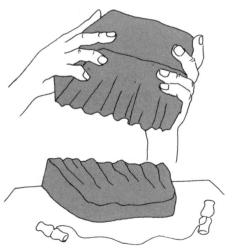

2C: The projecting clay being lifted prior to being slammed down onto the other clay. Note that both cut surfaces face the operator and that the two halves of the top surface now face each other. *Stage 3*

potters find it better to break off a handful of the newly-softened clay, squeeze it through the fingers until the clay is evenly-soft, then repeat this with another handful until all the clay has been so treated. The clay is then kneaded ready for use. This procedure takes time but it is well worth the trouble and some people really enjoy handling clay in this way!

3. It must be well-mixed so that both the colour and the texture of the clay are even and air is excluded. The latter is particularly important if the clay is to be used for throwing on the wheel. One good method of achieving an even, air-free clay, is to wedge it then knead it. In many cases only kneading is necessary.

Kneading

If the clay is reasonably well mixed without wedging, kneading only is necessary. If the clay has been wedged it should be even in texture but it is unlikely that all the bubbles and pockets of air will have been excluded. Kneading is, therefore, an essential process before the clay is used for pot making.

Method

Choose a strong bench such as that recommended for wedging with a slightly absorbent top or use a sheet of absorbent board. The ideal table is one that stands about 60 cm (24 in) high, for much of the energy used comes from the back-and-forth swaying movement of the body and not from the arm muscles. A lump of clay about 10 kg (22 lbs) is a convenient and easily managed size to use, although amounts ranging from 3 kg (6 lbs) to 18 kg (40 lbs) can be kneaded. At first, kneading can be exhausting but once the basic technique has been grasped and the weight of the body is used and not the arm muscles, it becomes quite a pleasant task. It is well worth practising this essential procedure until it is mastered, particularly if pots are to be made on the wheel, for they will not be made unless the clay is properly kneaded! Some potters consider that it takes two to three days to master kneading so part-time potters take heart!

There are two methods of kneading: *Bull's Head* and *Japanese Spiral Kneading*. The former is initially easier, the latter more efficient. The beginner is advised to use the Bull's Head method first, then progress to spiral kneading.

Bull's Head Kneading

a) Take a lump of clay 7–10 kg (15–22 lbs) in weight.

b) Press down with the heels of both hands, keeping the underside of the lump rounded, so that it rocks on the bench and does not stick.

c) Pull the clay forward with the fingers and repeat (b). The clay will gradually move toward the operator, rolling round within itself. The name Bull's Head will be apparent from the shape of the elongated form that results.

d) The clay is then stood on end and processes (b) and (c) repeated.

Japanese Spiral Kneading

a) Take a conical lump of clay about 7–10 kg (15–22 lbs).

b) Roll the base on the bench so that it is rounded.

c) Place the right hand on top, the left hand below.

d) Press down and then slightly away from the body with the heel of the right hand and the ball of the thumb of the left hand.

e) Lift the clay and repeat (d), introducing a slight swing or twist of the hands from the right to the left.

f) Repeat rhythmically for about five minutes, by which time about 150 turns should have been completed.

g) Give the clay about six more turns, easing the amount of pressure on each turn so that a neat, rounded lump is formed.

h) Check the kneading by cutting the lump in half with a wire to see if it is even in colour and texture and free from air bubbles. If it is unsatisfactory more kneading is required.

Some potters find it easier and/or more satisfactory to spiral the clay in the opposite direction.

The clay is now ready for cutting into lumps for use. If the clay is to be used on the wheel care should be taken not to join lots of small pieces of clay as this may well result in air being trapped, thus making the kneading a waste of time.

So, assuming that the clay has been well prepared, pot making can then commence.

Non-homogenous Wedging

This method of mixing is ideal for mixing clays, particularly if two differ-

Plate 6. Chinese T'ang dynasty (A.D. 618–906) earthenware bowl. Thrown, with red and white clays mixed to obtain a marbled effect, and a honey glaze.

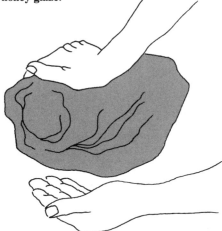

Fig. 3. Kneading
The partly kneaded clay, showing the position of the right hand, the spiral formation of the clay and the left hand ready to take its place next to the right hand.

ent clay bodies are to be mixed together or if large quantities of clay are to be prepared or reclaimed (10 kg/22 lbs plus).

It is basically a method of slicing and slamming the clay back together. A strong table with a slightly absorbent top is essential. Plastic topped tables are easy to clean but clay sticks to them when being worked, so at least one wooden or preferably slate- or concrete-topped bench is necessary in the workshop. The slate or marble top of an old wash-stand placed on a strong, flat table makes a good wedging bench.

Method
1. The clay is slammed onto the bench so that it projects over the edge of the bench.
2. It is cut in half using a wire with an upward slicing movement, the body and legs preventing the clay from falling.
3. The projecting clay is then turned over, lifted above the head and brought down with force onto the other half so that the two wire cut surfaces lie one above the other facing the operator.

4. The clay is then turned over and given a half a turn (90°) placing it on the bench so that it projects over the bench as in Fig. 2A. The process is then repeated for about a quarter of an hour, or until the clay is thoroughly mixed and of even texture.

Pinch Pots

This method is ideal for all beginners from infants to adults. It is ideal for getting the feel of clay; it is a method used by early man to make everyday, useful vessels and continues to be used by contemporary potters. I have found that some folks condemn pinch pots as mere child's play. I think this is wrong for two reasons. Firstly, superb little pots can be made by this method and secondly to make a more sophisticated type of pinch pot requires considerable skill and feeling for the clay.

Suitable clays

Most clays are suitable for pinch pots, ranging from white, delicate porcelain to heavily grogged clays such as Cranks Mixture and Saggar Marl. Whichever clay is chosen it must be plastic and suitably soft. Only practice will indicate how soft or firm a clay needs to be for a particular use. As always the clay should be kneaded before use.

Method of making pinch pots

1. Break off or cut with a wire, a piece of clay about 250 gms ($\frac{1}{2}$ lb) in weight.
2. By hitting the clay and rotating it in the hands make a sphere about 5 cm (2 in) in diameter. An easy size comparison is that of a tennis ball.
Note: *Do not handle the clay unless it involves a making process as the warmth of the hands will dry the surface of the clay and so cause surface cracking.*
3. Hold the clay in the palm of the left hand (for right-handed potters) and press the thumb of the right hand into the centre of the clay. Continue pressing with the thumb until it is about 5 mm ($\frac{1}{4}$ in) short of going right through. It is sometimes helpful to rotate the clay ball as the thumb is pressed into it.
4. Starting at the bottom of the pot squeeze the clay between the thumb and the fingers of the right hand so making the bottom 'course' of the pot about 5 mm ($\frac{1}{4}$ in) thick.

The left hand supports the pot as the right hand moves around the pot.
5. The right hand then moves up the pot

21

POT-MAKING WITHOUT A WHEEL

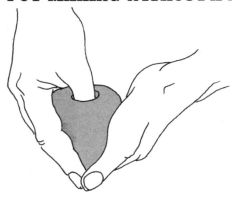

Fig. 4. Making a pinch pot
4A: The clay is held in the left hand while the clay is squeezed between the thumb and the fingers of the right hand.

4B: The stages in making a pinch pot. Note the way the base of the pot is first thinned before working up the pot.

and the next 'course' is squeezed until it is the same thickness as the first.

This process is repeated until the walls of the pot are an even thickness. The shape of the pot should be considered at all times and action taken to obtain the required shape. The direction of the right thumb, whether it is at 90° to the base or sloping out, determines the basic shape of the pinch pot. It is far easier to stretch out and widen a pot than it is to narrow it so it is as well to keep it fairly narrow at the rim. A slight squeezing with the left hand can help this to be achieved.

At all times make the squeezing action of the right hand rhythmic and not haphazard.

Rhythm in our work has all too often ceased in the Western World, whereas many African and South American peoples retain this essential rhythm and even appear to dance around their pots.
6. When the walls of the pot are of even thickness the final shaping can take place. The base of the pot can be gently tapped on a bench to make it a more

stable shape and a decorative rim made if so desired. Once the method of making a simple pot has been mastered there are many interesting projects to pursue. Here are some such projects but there are many other possible variations and additions to those described.

(1) Two Pinch Pots joined together
Make two pinch pots of the same wall thickness and size. The rims must not be less than 5 mm ($\frac{1}{4}$ in) thick. Cross-hatch the rims—that is, roughen the surfaces to be joined by scratching them with a piece of hacksaw blade. Paint with slurry (slushy wet clay) and press the two rims together.

Hold the pot with one hand and join the two sections together by scraping with the fingernail or hack-saw blade until the joint is barely visible. The resulting egg-shape can then be rolled on the bench and hit with a flat stick until the chosen form is made. Indentations can be made at this stage as can the addition of decorative coils and pellets of clay.

The form is remarkably strong until a hole is cut into it. The hole can be cut with a sharp, pointed knife or by using a twist drill held in the fingers. Some projects made in this way are:
a) **Small vases** Join two pots, shape, cut hole.
b) **Pebble forms** Join two pots, shape by rolling, beating and by pressing in smooth dents, cut hole.
c) **Burst pots** Join two pots, using fairly soft clay. Roll on the bench till spherical. Place near to the edge of the bench. Give the sphere a short, sharp blow with the clenched little finger.

In many cases this results in an interesting form with rough edges where

Fig. 5. Burst pots. One pot has been made into a fish.

the air has burst through the wall of the sphere. When fired with a dry glaze these pots make fascinating groups, well worth the noise involved in the making!
d) **Fish** Make a series of 'burst pots'. Some of the results will probably suggest open-mouthed fish. Pellets of clay can be applied with slurry to make the eyes, and simple fins can be made by pinching out pieces of clay which can then be joined onto the body with slurry.
e) **Landscapes** Make a sphere by joining two pinch pots and rolling on the bench. Arrange small coils and pellets of clay on a piece of newspaper so making trees, flowers and hills. Ensure that they overlap each other by at least a small amount 3 mm ($\frac{1}{8}$ in). Gently roll a rolling pin over the landscape so that the various pieces join together but not so that all the pattern is lost. While still damp, peel the 'landscape' from the paper and join it to the sphere. Make a small hole in the base or else the sphere is likely to burst or crack.
f) **Parcels** Join two pinch pots and roll into a smooth form. Roll out soft clay into thin coils, (3 mm/$\frac{1}{8}$ in or less). Wrap the coils around the sphere, making a pattern suggesting a string around a parcel or perhaps a ball of string. Roll the sphere, complete with the applied coils until they are well joined together and the coils are slightly squashed but not made invisible.
g) **Piggy Banks** Join two pinch pots, roll and beat them into a large egg form. Using slurry add a piece of clay and model it for the snout. In the same way add four stout legs, the ears and a tail. When the pig is leather-hard, that is, firm enough to keep its shape but soft enough to make an indentation with the thumb nail, use a sharp knife to cut out the money slot. Beware, the clay will shrink by about one tenth so make the slot a little over size.
h) **Owls** Join two pinch pots, then roll and beat them into an elongated egg form. Gently tap one end to make a base. Add a beak, eyes and ears. The eyes can be carved into the surface or added. Use a piece of pointed wood or a modelling tool to impress a pattern suggesting feathers. Feet may be added. The completed owl can either remain as an amusing model, in which case a hole must be made in the base, or it can be

made into a money box by cutting a slot between the ears.

Many other forms and animals such as rhinos and hippos can be made in a similar way.

It is worth noting that models or pots which are built up from sections are best dried slowly as this lessens the risk of the various sections coming apart due to varying rates of contraction.

A pinch pot is an excellent start when a larger coil pot with a small base is to be made. The pinch pot should be made and allowed to become firm before the coils are added as this will reduce the risk of the pot collapsing as the weight of additional coils is added.

Teachers, ranging from primary through to the adult level, find pinch pots an excellent way of introducing clay and its plastic potential. Pinch pots should not be regarded as only suitable for young children, and poor standards of craftsmanship should not be accepted. By taking a craftsman-like approach and expecting a high standard of work the results will be very satisfying.

Coil Pots

Early man used pinch pots when small pots were required and coil pots when larger pots were demanded. The earliest developments in pottery seem to have been in the Near East in such ancient civilisations as Egypt and Mesopotamia in about 6000 B.C. It was only when people ceased to be nomadic and began to settle in villages and towns that any great technical or cultural advance could be made.

The earliest Near Eastern pots that have been found were made of a fairly open rough clay which had only been fired to a low temperature, 450°C–700°C. Such pots were built by coiling and frequently resembled vessels made of other materials such as stone and animal skins.

From about 3500 B.C. the Mesopotamians used some kind of wheel or turntable. These wheels were usually what is known as 'slow-wheels', that is they were turned round slowly, sometimes by an assistant, so making the placing of one coil upon another much easier. We use banding-wheels in much the same way.

The Chinese culture was not at this

Plate 7. Very ancient Chinese earthenware pot, *c.* 2,000 B.C. Hand-built and unglazed.

Plate 8. Chinese pre-dynastic mortuary vase dated somewhere between 2000 and 1500 B.C. Earthenware, it is hand-built, unglazed and painted with coloured slips.

23

POT-MAKING WITHOUT A WHEEL

time as advanced as the Near East although in the centuries preceding the Christian Era China was to equal and overtake the Near East.

The funerary jars made in China about 2000 B.C. with their superb spiral decoration painted with black and red earth pigments must surely rank as some of the most beautiful pots ever produced. These pots, which were coiled have, like the later pots of the Near East, a smooth, burnished surface. This is the result of using more refined clays and of coating the completed pot with a fine liquid clay known as slip. When this was almost dry it was burnished with a smooth pebble or bone. Different coloured slips were also used to paint on the decoration of the wares produced in the Near East from about 2000 B.C.

Coiling was also used in Minoan Crete (1450–1400 B.C.) to make the huge storage vessels found in the palaces at Knossos. They stand 1 m (3 ft) high and more and many have coils applied to the outside, like rope, as decoration. Such pots are still made by coiling and throwing, the potter having ten or more in the making at any one time so that he can work on one while the others firm-up, thus avoiding collapsing. He applies a coil, then has the pot turned by an assistant while he throws the coil into shape.

Many African peoples, notably the Nigerians, and South American Indians still make superb pots by coiling. To watch a potter such as Ladi Kwali from Nigeria build in a couple of hours a coil pot about 60 cm high (2 ft) which is symmetrical, quite thin and so beautifully balanced in form, is sheer magic.

The Peruvian Indians, who continue to hand-build their pots, only take half-an-hour to make a cooking vessel about 45 cm (18 in) high which is superbly thin and even. They, like the Nigerians, walk around their pots as they work. All their movements are rhythmic and flowing so that they appear almost to dance around their work. This rhythm is essential if the pot is to grow evenly and have any vitality.

Thanks to the re-introduction of the coiling technique to Western potters and Art Schools by such people as

Plate 9. This hand-built Egyptian earthenware piece was made over 4,000 years ago. It has a floral design in red slip.

Helen Pincombe, many potters now use coiling, either wholly or in part, to make their pots. The work of Ruth Duckworth, who makes such strong forms in stoneware; Alan Wallwork, whose coiled pebble forms have influenced the work of many school potteries; Elizabeth Fritsch, who makes superb asymmetrical pots decorated with slip; and the fascinating animals of Rosemary Wren are all excellent examples of the use of coiling by modern potters.

It is well worth studying the work or photographs of such potters as well as the work made by peoples in the past, using coiling methods, before starting a coiled pot of your own.

Suitable Clays

Most clays are suitable for coiling. The one selected should accept the proposed firing temperature and be reasonably plastic. If large pots of 30 cm plus (1 ft) are contemplated it is best to use a grogged clay, such as Cranks Mixture,

Saggar Marl or a throwing clay into which has been kneaded some coarse grog (30's–dust) or sand. This will help the pot to firm up quickly as building proceeds, for a grogged clay contains less water by volume than an ungrogged.

The clays used by some of the Peruvian Indian potters are very crumbly, open and non-plastic, yet they stand up so well that a pot of about 60 cm (2 ft) high can be made within half an hour.

If a fine clay, such as red earthenware or porcelain is used, care must be taken to dry out the completed pot slowly and to allow the pot to firm-up during the making process so that it does not collapse due to being too wet.

Method of making

(a) Although it may be helpful to draw the profile of the pot that is to be made or at least know in your mind the shape and size of the pot to be made, keep in mind that coiling is eminently suited to developing, discovering, or changing shapes. One advantage of having a set design in mind is the knowledge of the possible problems that can arise while working on a certain shape. This is true for most Peruvian and African potters who make only three or four basic shapes all their lives.

b) Knead the clay well, at the same time ensuring that it is fairly firm but not so firm that a strip of 2.5 cm (1 in) diameter cracks when bent into a gentle curve.

c) Make the base of the pot. If it is to be a small base (10 cm (4 in) or less) a large pinch pot can be made and then gently tapped on the bench top until a base of the required size is achieved. Small cracks are soon smoothed out with the fingers or the back of the finger nail. If the base is to be larger, or not circular, a slab of clay can be rolled out or tapped out with the hand, karate-style, onto a board or piece of hessian of suitable size. The base should be the same thickness as the intended walls of the pot which will depend on the size of the proposed pot, 1 cm (½ in approx) is a reasonable thickness for pots ranging between 15 cm and 45 cm (6 and 18 in). The disc of clay or whatever shape is required, is now cut from the slab of prepared clay and placed on a board, upon which it can remain until the pot is completed.

Note: *The bases of most good coil pots*

Fig. 6. Coiling

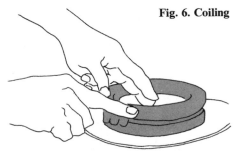

6A: The first coil is joined to the base. The left hand supports the coil while the first finger of the right hand presses and scrapes the coil onto the base. *Stage (e)*

6B: The second coil is placed inside the first coil and squeezed into position. Subsequent coils are joined in the same way. *Stage (f)*

6C: Recently joined coils are squeezed to the required thickness and shape. The left hand rotates the banding wheel. *Stage (g)*

6D: The outside of the completed pot is scraped with a piece of hacksaw blade. *Stage (h)*

are remarkably small yet beginners seem to think that a pot over 15 cm high (6 in) requires an enormous base. It is as well to be aware of this common fault and make the bases smaller than might be thought necessary for the height of pot.

d) Roll out a coil. This is best done by cutting off a piece of the kneaded clay and squeezing it in the hands into a fat if rather rough coil. This is then placed on a bench, allowing ample space for rolling and the coil to stretch.

The coil should be rolled with the whole length of the hands, from finger tips to wrists. The movement should be long and even with a slight outward movement of the hands from the centre to the ends of the coil.

When the coil is approximately the required diameter, about 2 cm (1 in) for most pots, only roll those sections of the coil that are still too thick. Some potters like to roll out a good supply of coils before building their pots, others roll one at a time. It is, in my opinion, easier to get an evenly made pot and much quicker, if fat coils, 2 cm (1 in) plus, are used than if small worm-like coils are used.

e) Join the first coil to the base. Place the coil on top of the base, nipping off the ends in a wedge shape so that they can be overlapped.

Do not use slurry or water to join the coils. Use a finger to join the coil firmly to the base, both inside and out.

25

POT-MAKING WITHOUT A WHEEL

It is helpful if the base is placed on a banding wheel, whirler or small table so that the pot can either be turned or the potter walk around the pot.

f) Join the second (and subsequent) coil by placing it on the inside of the preceding coil and gently squeeze it into place. Nip off the end into a wedge-shape so that the ends can overlap.

Do not spiral a continuous coil as this will lead to the pot leaning over to one side.

g) Thin the coil which has just been placed into position by squeezing it between the thumb and fingers, remembering to work rhythmically and to keep the pot growing into the required shape.

h) Continue joining on coils, squeezing them to the required thickness and keeping the pot in shape until the required height and form are achieved. If this is not possible in one day keep the pot damp by wrapping it in plastic sheeting.

If the pot has any tendency to bulge or collapse, due to the clay being too wet to support the weight above it, allow the pot to dry a little so that it is firm but not too dry to shape.

i) Smooth the surface of the pot either when it is up to its full height or if the neck is to be narrow, stop building while it is still possible to get a hand inside the pot and smooth the pot as far as it has gone. Always smooth the coils together with an up, down or crossways movement and not with a horizontal movement as this will cause the coils to stretch and the pot to collapse.

A piece of coarse hack-saw blade is very useful for the initial smoothing as it drags the clay from the high spots to the hollows. The surface is then soon smoothed with the fingers. Another way of shaping the pot is to beat it with a flat stick. This, like using a hack-saw blade, makes a distinctive pattern which can either be left or smoothed out.

j) The pot is now complete except for decorating, firing and glazing. If it is a large pot, 45 cm (18 in) high plus, dry it out slowly so as to avoid cracking.

Projects using the coiling method of construction

Apart from making pots of the traditional open top type many other interesting forms can be made by coiling, some are listed with comment,

Plate 10. This stoneware cider jar is the work of a 15-year-old student. Made by coiling

but in all cases ensure that the clay is suitable for the job and that it is well-kneaded.

1. Asymmetrical pots

It is probably technically easier to make a symmetrical pot but pots with bases that are oval or irregular in shape and/or walls that are distinctly asymmetrical can look superb if well considered and made with due craftsmanship.

They are made in the same way as described for symmetrical pots. Extra care should be taken to ensure that the shape does not get out of hand or an over-bulbous shape collapse.

Gentle indentations can be made when the pot is built and still soft enough to allow stretching and re-shaping.

Take care that the pot remains stable and not over-weighted on one side, for this will make building the pot difficult, render it impracticable for use and run the risk of it collapsing during a stoneware glaze firing.

2. Lamp bases

Pots with suitably narrow necks and stable bases can make excellent table lamps. Symmetrical and asymmetrical forms are equally suitable if the following requirements are considered when designing the form and during making.

Plate 11. Another example of school work. This coiled cider jar has a semi-matt blue glaze.

Plate 12. Landscape pot by Anne James. Porcelain, it was thrown, modelled and cut. Such pots can also be made by pinching.

The pot must be stable even when a light socket and shade are fitted. This means that the base must not be very narrow or the pot extremely light. However, this does not imply that the pot has to be dumpy and nearly solid!

The fact that the pot will have a lampshade above it should be considered aesthetically as well as when considering the pot's stability. A common fault is to have a short, dumpy pot with a large shade above it which, to say the least, lacks grace.

The opening at the top of the pot needs to be of a suitable size to accept a standard light fitting. The fittings sold for adapting a bottle into a lamp are relatively inexpensive and suitable. If the opening is 2 cm ($\frac{3}{4}$ in) in diameter when the pot is built it will be the correct size when the pot has been fired and has consequently shrunk. If a large opening is made the light fitting will require packing with cork so it is as well to make the opening 2 cm ($\frac{3}{4}$ in) when building the pot.

The flex is best threaded through the pot and out of a hole made in the wall of the pot, near to the base. The hole should be about 1 cm ($\frac{3}{8}$ in) in diameter, be in the wall of the pot just above the base and preferably made with a twist drill, held in the hand when the pot is leather-hard. Do not make the hole in the base of the pot unless it is to have feet; otherwise it will rock about on the flex.

Most types of pot, such as slab and thrown pots, can be adapted into lamp bases if the points just mentioned are considered before and during the making process.

3. Pebble forms

Many rock-like sculptural forms can be included under this heading. A pot which is approximately spherical in shape is coiled, completely closing up the neck, using a disc of clay to fill the final opening. The resultant form, filled with trapped air, is remarkably strong and will tolerate a lot of beating, scraping and shaping provided the clay is firm enough so as not to be floppy, but not *too* firm, otherwise the clay will split and resist re-shaping.

The final result could be round and flowing like a river-worn boulder or angular and sharp like a piece of freshly-quarried building stone.

The surface can also range from a smooth burnished finish to a rough scraped finish.

It is advisable not to cut a hole or holes in the form until all the shaping has been completed and the clay is fairly firm but not dry. The openings can then be made with a twist drill, a sharp knife or a strong needle.

If the form is not to have a visible opening, to make the form functional or as part of the overall design, a hole must be made in the base so that the trapped air can escape. Failure to make an opening will cause the air to expand during firing which will in turn break the pot open!

4. Human and animal figures

An excellent change from making pots —yet using the coiling technique—is to make figures. This idea has been pursued by Rosemary Wren, who makes her superb and sometimes amusing animal figures by coiling. She varies the basic coiling technique in that she pinches round coils so that they are triangular thus allowing her to build a thinly walled pot yet giving her plenty of clay with which to join coil to coil.

The basic coiling method already described is quite adequate but it is worth remembering that many variations are possible and can be ideal for one potter but not another. Many students seem to enjoy making figures, particularly youngsters of 14 years and under who are not yet able to appreciate the more abstract quality of pots, considering them purely in terms of containers.

The type and form of figure is limited by the behaviour of clay when it is plastic and when it is being fired. An obviously unsuitable figure would be a giraffe for the long legs would be extremely difficult to build and they would probably bend during a stoneware glaze firing! Ideal forms are those which are basically rounded and have a large base area. Elephants, hippos, sitting cats and dogs, cows that are lying down, stumpy legged fat dwarfs, crinolined ladies, and many other forms if they are stylised to avoid delicate legs, etcetera, are ideal projects.

Rosemary Wren has made superb birds, such as pigeons, by simplifying the forms yet capturing their essential characteristics. Before starting to coil the chosen form, careful thought must be given to the essential characteristics of the figure or animal so that these might be captured in the modelling— in the case of some human figures it may well lead to caricature. Always ensure, as has been mentioned, that the base is of a reasonable size and not too small to support any subsequent weight above it.

It is not essential to have a base so the first coil can be placed on a board making the required base outline for the figure. In the case of a figure standing on legs these will have to be made either by coiling small cylinders or by making small pinch pots. The legs are then positioned and the first coil of the body used to link them together.

Coils are then carefully built up, squeezing them to the required thickness and shape as building proceeds. Some figures will require building up more at one end than the other—such as the neck and head of a cow or pigeon —in which case the body should be completed leaving an opening for the neck so that this can be built up with small coils.

Always take care that the clay is not too wet and allow the partly-completed figure to firm up at the first sign of collapse.

When the basic form has been coiled features such as the face, arms, legs, hair and clothing can be modelled onto the body, taking care that the body is still leather-hard or wetter and that any additions are well applied, using slurry on the surfaces to be joined.

The surface can be carved and different textures used to add character and interest to the completed figure.

Due to the amount of joining involved, the figure should be dried slowly so as to avoid cracking at the joints.

Coiling can be used for many other projects based upon those mentioned and can be combined with slabbing techniques which are discussed in the next chapter. An example of such a composite pot would be a round neck coiled onto a square base made by slabbing.

SLAB POTS AND OTHER PROJECTS

Slab Pots

The earliest slabs were probably the roofing tiles and writing tablets of the ancient Near East. Such tablets include those found at Tell 'Umar in Iraq dating from about 1700 B.C., which give a formula for a copper-lead glaze. Such slabs were, like early building bricks, seldom fired. Only pots which were to be used as containers were fired and it would appear that slabs were not used to construct pots.

Among the earliest slab-built constructions are the model homes, cooking stoves, farms and utensils which were buried in China during the Han dynasty (206 B.C.–A.D. 200) with the bodies of important people. They were obviously intended to accompany the spirits of the dead into the next world. The models were superbly made, showing, in considerable detail, how buildings of the time were constructed, including the tiling of roofs, and also the animals kept. The models were fired to a low temperature and coloured with pigment. They were not usually glazed. The Chinese continued to make slab pots in comparatively small numbers including, during the Ming dynasty (1368–1644), square bottles made in porcelain and highly decorated. Similar bottles were made in Japanese 'Arita' ware about 1700.

The Japanese have been making specialised slab pots since the 17th century for the Tea Ceremony, for growing the miniature trees, Bonsai, and for flower arrangements. All are associated with Zen Buddhism, their shape and proportions are a specialised study but in most cases they are wide shallow dishes of simple form and fired from the low Raku temperatures of 700°C to stoneware temperatures of 1,300°C.

European potters seldom used slabbing techniques, preferring coiling, then throwing, and finally moulding methods. This is perhaps somewhat surprising as tile making was energetically pursued from medieval times onwards. Many twentieth century potters have used, and continue to use, slab techniques—alone or in combination with coiling, throwing or modelling, to build their pots.

In addition to the work of established potters many interesting slab-built pots/

sculptures are being made by Art School students and a visit to their diploma shows is usually well worth while. They are a source of ideas and in most cases they give an indication of the high standard of craftsmanship and finish obtainable.

Suitable Clays

Any clay suited to the firing temperature and the proposed glazes can be used for slabbing. Having said that, it must be born in mind that a slab pot has to undergo considerable stress during the drying and firing stages, therefore it is better to use clays that are particularly co-operative during the drying and firing stages.

If earthenware is being used the problem is reduced to the drying-out stage because there is far less likelihood of the clay warping during firing than there is with the higher temperatures of a stoneware firing. So for earthenware the greatest danger of cracking and warping is during the drying-out stage. This can be overcome by ensuring that the completed pot dries out very slowly, that is over a period of one or even two

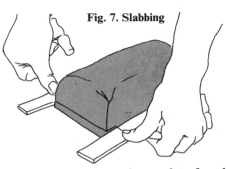
Fig. 7. Slabbing

Plate 13. This delightful group of seven houses dates from the northern Wei dynasty in China, A.D. 385-535. Earthenware, slab built and modelled, such pieces were buried in the graves of prominent people.

cracking during the drying stage and warping during high firing are to a large extent overcome.

If a grogged clay is not stocked a coarse stoneware grog (-30's $+60$'s mesh) should be kneaded into a finer clay that is suitable for the required firing temperature. The grog is kneaded in by spreading some dampened grog on the kneading bench and kneading a large lump of clay (10 kg/22 lbs) on the grog until it has been taken up by the clay. Spread more grog on the bench until the clay contains a generous amount of grog yet is still plastic and not too open and crumbly for use.

Whichever clay is used it must be well-kneaded, so as to be free of air pockets, and of even consistency. A firm clay, rather drier than would be used for pinch, coil or thrown pots is often more suitable for cutting slabs and reduces waiting time at later stages.

Method of Making

a) Never start making a slab pot before preparing paper or cardboard templates or at least working out the exact sizes that the various sections need to be. If the pot is to be square-based only one template needs to be made, that being the one for the sides. The sides being identical the same template is used four times. A template is not necessary for the base.

If the sides of the pot are to be curved the templates must also be curved.

If the pot has sides of two different dimensions, such as a flat bottle, two templates will have to be prepared. Once the templates are ready the next stage can begin.

b) Having prepared the clay by kneading make it into a shape from which the largest required slab can be cut. Always ensure that the block is plenty big enough so as to avoid the annoyance of not having sufficient prepared clay.

A square pot will require a lump of clay which is square in section and high enough to cut the four sides, a base and a top if required (Fig. 7A). Place the block of clay on a clean, dry bench top. Place a slat of wood on each side of the block. The thickness of the slats required will

7A: A slice of clay is cut using two slats of wood and a taut cutting wire. *Stage (b)*

7B: Cutting out the side of a pot using a card template, a slat of wood and a knife. The slat of wood prolongs the life of the template and gives a more accurate edge. *Stage (d)*

7C: Mitring the vertical edges using a wooden guide cut at 45°. *Stage (e)*

weeks for larger pots. The following comments on clay for stoneware slab pots can also be applied to earthenware with advantage but remember that by altering the clay body the glaze might not fit and crazing result.

Stoneware slab pots can present difficulties during the drying and the firing stages. If a fine clay with a high contraction rate is used there is a danger of the joints opening or even a crack appearing in one of the slabs. If a fine clay is to be used for a good reason such as the inlaying of a slip decoration great care must be taken to dry the pot slowly. Porcelain slab pots are particularly difficult to make, due to cracking during the drying stage and a strong tendency to warp during firing. Only skilled potters with a philosophical approach to disappointments should tackle porcelain slab pots!

The best clays to use are grogged clays. Heavily-grogged clays, such as Saggar Marl and Cranks Mixture, being particularly good, for they have a low contraction rate and will stand up well when fired to 1,300°C. So the danger of

SLAB POTS AND OTHER PROJECTS

7D: Cross hatching and applying slurry prior to assembling the sides. *Stage (f)*

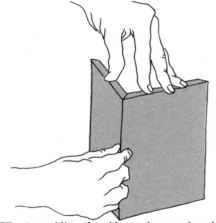

7E: Assembling the sides and squeezing the mitred edges together. *Stage (g)*

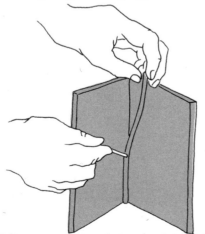

7F: Inserting a fillet of clay to reinforce the joint. *Stage (g)*

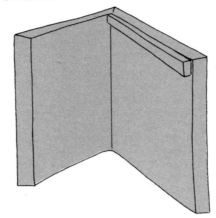

7G: A reinforcing strip applied at the rim of an open box to prevent warping. *Stage (k)*

vary with the size of pot to be made (6 mm to 1 cm ($\frac{1}{4}$ in to $\frac{3}{8}$ in) being suitable for pots up to 30 cm (1 ft) high.

Take a cutting wire and keeping it taut across the slats and pressed down with the thumbs, draw it through the block of clay.

Lift the block from the cut slab and again place it down on the bench and cut another slab. Repeat this until sufficient slabs have been cut.

I find the method described gives more even slabs in a shorter time than does rolling out clay on a piece of hessian using a rolling pin and slats as thickness guides. Some people claim it is easier to roll out the clay as less clay has to be kneaded, but I find that the saving is outweighed by the rolling required and a slightly inferior result.

c) The cut slabs are now placed on a clean absorbent sheet or flat wooden board, and allowed to firm-up. The slabs should be firm enough to support themselves when stood up but not so dry that they crack when slightly curved. A curved-sided pot will require slightly damper slabs.

It is hopeless attempting to assemble slabs if they are wet and floppy or so dry that they will come apart at the joints. If the slices are to be stored from one day or week to another they should be placed on damp wooden, not absorbent, boards, the boards and slabs carefully wrapped in plastic and stored in a cool place.

d) When the slabs have firmed-up use the prepared template to cut out the sides. Leave the base and top oversize. It is better to use a rule or slat of wood along the edge of the template as shown in Fig 7B, as this prolongs the life of the template and gives a better edge for the knife. The knife should be thin and sharp.

e) The vertical edges to be joined are now mitred, that is cut at 45°, rather like the corners of a picture frame. This can be done using a strip of wood cut at 45° as a guide or if such an aid is not available score a line on the slab parallel with the edge and the same distance as the slab is thick away from the edge. Place a ruler or straight slat along the scored line and by cutting from this line to the edge of the slab on the bench, a 45° mitre will be cut. Mitre all the vertical edges in this way but do not mitre the top, bottom or base.

f) Cross-hatch the mitred edges to give the surface a key that will aid joining and coat the edges with slurry made from the clay being used to build the pot.

g) Assemble two sides by standing one against the other. Check that they are at 90° to each other and gently squeeze the mitred edges together from the outside of the pot. Some of the slurry should ooze out. If the pot is 15 cm (6 in) tall or more it is advisable to roll out a thin coil of clay, about 6 mm ($\frac{1}{4}$ in) diameter and press it into the angle made by the two sides (see Fig. 7E).

Such fillets should be used to reinforce all the joints at which it is possible to get.

h) Join the other two sides so that all the sides are joined and the interior angles reinforced with fillets.

i) Stand the completed and joined sides of the pot onto the slab cut for the base. Score around the outside of the pot. Remove the sides and cross-hatch and slurry where they made contact with the base. Replace the sides onto the base, carefully pressing them down so that the slurry oozes out of the join.

j) With a sharp knife held against the sides of the pot trim the base to size. Ensure that the base is well-joined to the sides, smooth one into the other where necessary.

k) If a top is to be added this should be applied in the same way as the base. If, however, the pot is to be open at the top it is advisable to place a reinforcing strip the same thickness as the walls of the pot and between 6 mm ($\frac{1}{4}$ in) and 1 cm ($\frac{1}{2}$ in) deep around the inside of the rim (see illustration). All surfaces to be joined must be cross-hatched and coated with slurry. This will help prevent warpage during a stoneware firing.

l) The slab pot is now complete except for any scraping or smoothing that is considered desirable. A Surform blade is a useful tool for trimming the pot when it is still leather-hard and a piece of hack-saw blade is equally useful as a scraper and smoother.

Any slip, incised or applied decoration should be added while the pot is still damp.

m) The pot should now be allowed to dry out slowly. If the clay used is fine, with a high shrinkage rate, it is doubly important that the pot dries out slowly. The pot can either be placed in a damp cupboard for a day or two, then placed in a cool draught-free area until it has dried out, or wrapped in plastic sheeting (which should be air-tight) for a couple of days and then loosened bit by bit over a period of a week. Never place a damp slab pot on a warm kiln to dry or else the joints will come apart.

Projects using slabbing as the main method of construction

In addition to straight and curved sided vases and bottles many other vessels both useful and decorative can be made.

1. Multi-sectional pots In theory a dozen or more slabs could be used to build up a bottle or straight sided pot. Considerable skill and patience are required but if the proportions of the pot are pleasing the result can be most impressive and worthwhile.

I have seen octagonal bottles based on Korean pots of the Silla dynasty which are beautiful as well as being considerable feats of patience.

If a pot has more than four sides the mitres will not be cut at 45° but at the equivalent of 180° divided by the number of sides to be assembled. For example, for an octagonal pot (8 sides) 180° is divided by 8 giving 22½°. This is always assuming that the pot is a regular geometric form with all the sides being of equal size.

If an irregular shape is to be made the best way to cut mitres is to offer up the sides one to the other, mark the mitre required on each slab then place the slab on the bench to cut the required mitres. An alternative method is to make a cardboard mock-up and measure the angles between each of the sides.

Complicated geometric forms, both regular and irregular can be constructed. For example, a duodecagon, which looks something like an angular sphere, could and has been used as the basis for a slab-built tea pot.

However, it is important that pots do not just become feats of skill best executed in another material but remain objects of beauty. Always take great care when drying a multi-sectional pot, a period of two weeks or so being desirable unless the clay used is known to be of a low contraction rate and generally very co-operative.

2. Bottles with thrown or coiled necks A tall, slender bottle or one that is a narrow rectangle in section, with a narrow, round neck, frequently make pleasing pots. It seems easier to make a pot of pleasing proportions if it has a small base and a narrow neck. Many beginners, being cautious, tend to make unpleasantly dumpy pots but that is not to say that pots with relatively large bases cannot be pleasing or in some cases even beautiful.

To produce a bottle make the slabbed part as already described, working with templates or at least a sketch of the

Plate 14. A striking stoneware piece by Anthony Hepburn (1967). Slab built, it is white with bright red enamel decoration on the tongues.

proposed pot. When this has been assembled and a thrown top is to be added, wrap it in plastic or put it in a damp cupboard while the top is thrown and allowed to firm-up until it is of similar consistency to the assembled base. Remember to throw the top so that it will fit the top of the base as well as considering the overall effect of the base plus top. When the top is ready for assembly cross-hatch and slurry all edges that are to be joined, press the top firmly into position, trim any surplus clay and complete any surface treatment such as scraping. If a coiled neck is to be applied in place of one that has been thrown there is no need to wrap the damp but completed walls of the pot in plastic. Instead, the coiled neck should be started by cross-hatching and slurrying the top of the walls and the first coil made from the same body and the slabs carefully positioned around the top making sure it is well attached to the walls. It may be difficult to use the large coils recommended for a coil pot, in which case use coils of a smaller diameter but do not squeeze them any thinner than the slabs used for the walls.

Continue coiling the neck, smoothing the inside as the work progresses for it will be difficult to get inside later if the neck is narrow. Always take care not to damage the walls of the pot by pressing down too hard, and use clay which is as dry as possible so as to avoid any danger of the neck contracting more than the walls, thus causing the two sections to crack apart.

When completed, dry out with care, remembering that any slip decoration and sprigging (applying a relief pattern) must be applied while the pot is damp and any carved decoration is best carried out at the leather-hard stage.

Pots of this sort are frequently ideal for decorating and it is well worth experimenting with different methods of decoration on such pots.

3. Lamp bases A slab pot with a narrow neck is soon adapted into a lamp base. Care must be taken when designing the pot to allow for the fact that a lamp shade will be above it and the base and the shade must complement each other and not look as though the base has just had an oversize hat dumped upon it. If the lamp, complete with shade, is not to be easily toppled,

SLAB POTS AND OTHER PROJECTS

care must be taken to have a sufficiently wide base for the height of the completed lamp. This does not mean that the only suitably stable shape is fat and dumpy but it does mean that the function of the pot must be considered as well as striving to make a form which has beauty.

The diameter of the top should be about 2 cm ($\frac{3}{4}$ in) when made so that after the pot has shrunk while drying and firing, a standard light socket made for fitting into a bottle top will fit the pot. A hole 6 mm ($\frac{1}{4}$ in) diameter should be made near to the base in the wall of the pot for the electric flex.

If the pot is to be decorated it is necessary to remember that it will be strongly lit from above. Incised decoration can be very effective as strong shadows and reflections from pooled glaze often result from this type of decoration.

As with all slab pots care must be taken to dry the pot slowly.

4. Boxes Square and rectangular boxes are really slab pots with lids. They can be superb objects having a feeling of preciousness and care about them or they can be more sculptural, direct and decorated. The approach is the same as described for a slab pot except that thought and care must be given to the lid fitting.

There are two basic methods used for lid fitting; two pots can be made with the same opening dimensions and a means of holding the lid in place such as four pellets of clay pressed into the corners of the base section or a small strip of clay can be placed on the inside edge of the base section so forming a flange over which fits the lid section.

If the lid is to be fairly thin and more than 5 cm (2 in) across there is some danger of sagging during a stoneware glaze firing.

The best way to overcome this danger is to make the lid slightly domed while the clay is damp so making a much stronger structure.

Another method is to make the walls and lid of the box thicker but even this will not prevent sagging if the lid is more than about 10 cm (4 in) across, whereas doming the lid is usually satisfactory for pots up to 30 cm (12 in) across.

Porcelain can be used to make boxes that will look delicate and precious. Great care is necessary when using porcelain, both during the making process and when drying the completed box. All work surfaces and tools must be clean so that the porcelain remains white and extra care must be taken to ensure that all the slabs that are to be joined are of equal consistency, not having one dryer than the others. The completed pot must be dried out with great care, allowing two weeks of gentle drying if cracking at the joints is to be avoided. Porcelain can be very effectively decorated at the leather-hard stage by incising with a sharp tool, such as a piece of bamboo cut to a chisel edge. The Chinese Sung dynasty pots frequently have such incised decoration in the form of flowers. The incision collects a slightly thicker layer of translucent glaze giving a quiet and subtle variation in colour.

Porcelain also gives a good light background if brush decoration is to be used. See the chapter on decoration.

More sculptural boxes can be made using a grogged clay. Boxes based upon the shape of treasure chests with miniature 'treasures' spilling out and various crustaceans such as shells and star-fish applied to the box can make an interesting and inventive project.

This requires both carefully planned work for the box and rather free sculptural work for the applied crustaceans.

5. Shallow dishes Shallow dishes for modern flower arrangements and for the growing of miniature Bonsai trees make useful projects.

The method of making is the same as described for a basic slab pot. If the dish is to be made in stoneware and is more than 10 cm (4 in) across it may be necessary to support the base in the centre. If the base is flat no additional support will be necessary, for the whole of the base will be supported by the kiln shelf, but if any kind of feet or foot ring are to be applied, as is quite usual with this kind of dish, a support must be added in the centre of the dish to prevent the base from sagging.

The feet of traditional Bonsai pots are frequently the only form of decoration on such pots. The feet also enable the pot to drain better and an adequate drainage hole or holes must be cut in the base during the assembly of the pot.

Both Bonsai pots for miniature trees, and dishes for flower arranging, are derived from the cultural practices of Japanese Zen Buddhism and both have strict traditions as to shape, proportion, decoration and glaze. Any student interested in such pots is advised to read more specialised publications on the subject but at the risk of over simplification of a complex cultural tradition, the pots are kept very simple, even severe, with a minimum of decoration.

Some books on modern flower arranging show very complicated pots, some of which are very difficult to make and are not really suitable projects for a potter.

However, many flower arranging societies like such pots. If attempting one

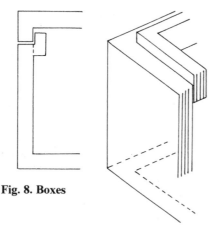

Fig. 8. Boxes

8A: A lid fitting, using strips of clay to form a continuous flange.

8B: A lid fitting, using a pellet of clay in each corner.

always ensure that the pot to be made is not likely to sag and warp in the firing. This is particularly important if stoneware, which is more inclined to warp, is being used.

Wrap-around pots

This method of making does not permit the wide range of shapes that can be made by coiling or throwing, but it does allow quite tall pots to be made in relatively short time. The method of making restricts the basic shapes made to tubes, either square or round, but the basic shape can be added to by coiling, slabbing or throwing, so considerably extending the range of pots that can be made using this method.

As far as I can ascertain there is no continuing tradition for wrap-around pots, although the method was used by the Han dynasty Chinese.

The method has been used with considerable success over the past twenty years, most art schools introducing it and many potters who hand-build using it, often in combination with other methods of making.

Some of the potters using it most effectively are Eileen Lewenstein. Dan Arbeid and James Campbell. The simple tube form has influenced many student potters by its directness and simplicity. The method of making is obvious. The decoration is an extension of the making method and the proportion of height to diameter gives the pot a feeling of lightness and stability.

Suitable clays The same basic requirements apply for wrap-around pots as for slab pots. That is, any well-prepared clay suitable for the intended firing range, preference being given to a clay with a low contraction rate so as to lessen the risk of cracking during drying out and firing. Porcelain can be used if great care is taken to dry the completed pot very slowly.

Some of the most effective wrap-around pots I have seen have been made with a fairly heavily grogged clay. This dries quickly, so shortening the making time, it has a pleasant surface texture over colour and it seldom cracks whilst drying or firing. It is only suitable for stoneware, so if earthenware is to be used some grog could be added to an earthenware body to reduce the shrinkage rate. The clay should be reasonably soft as for coiling, not firm as used for slab making. If the clay is too firm it will crack when wrapped around the tube.

Method of Making

1. Choose a tube or block around which the clay will be wrapped ensuring that a pot of sufficient height can be made with the tube. The full height of the

Plate 15. This stoneware tube pot was made by wrapping clay around a tube, then beating it with a stick. Iron oxide was rubbed into the unglazed exterior. It is the work of a 14-year-old student.

Fig. 9. Wrap-around pots

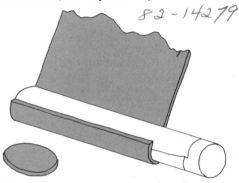

9A: The slice of clay cut ready for wrapping around tube, with a piece ready for the base.

9B: Wrapping the clay around the tube.

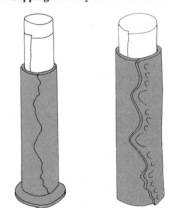

9C: The clay wrapped around the tube and placed on a base ready for trimming.
9D: The completed pot. The example has a decorative lapped edge.

tube does not have to be used. A source of suitable tubes is a local shop or store selling fabrics, for most fabrics are delivered wound round strong cardboard tubes. Wooden blocks can often be found on the scrap pile of a school woodwork shop or a timber merchant.

2. Prepare sufficient clay from which to cut or roll a slice of clay that will go around the tube and be of the required height. It is better to have some clay over than find there is insufficient.

If more than one pot is to be made it is easier to cut the slices from a prepared block of clay. This method gives a crisp slice and by cutting with a twisted wire various surface textures can be introduced. It is worth experimenting with such textures by moving the wire from side to side and up and down as it is pulled through the block of clay.

If the clay is rolled out instead of cutting from a block it must be placed on a piece of sheeting or hessian to prevent it sticking to the bench top. The sheet or hessian can be creased or lengths of string, rope or cloth arranged on the hessian so that an impressed decoration is made. The thickness of the slice will be determined by the height of the proposed pot.

3. Cut the slice so that it is the proposed height of the pot and cut one of the vertical edges. It is difficult to measure the required width of clay required at this stage so leave it generously wide to go around the circumference of the tube, with an untrimmed edge.

4. Wrap newspaper around the tube or block to prevent the clay sticking to it, which would make it impossible to remove the tube from the pot. The paper should be kept free of creases, not folded over the top or bottom of the tube and it can be kept in position with Sellotape, Scotch tape, etc. Failure to wrap the tube in this way will result in it being impossible to remove the tube without spoiling the pot. If the tube is left inside, the pot will crack as it contracts during drying.

5. Check that the slice is free to move on the bench, or peel it free from any sheeting or hessian. Carefully wrap the clay around the tube keeping one edge of the clay level with the base of the

tube. If a square block is used do not press the clay hard over the corners as this can cause the clay to crack.

Allow any surplus clay to overlap.

6. Using a sharp knife trim off the surplus clay. Take care not to squeeze or roll the partly completed pot as this will stretch the clay and make a rather sloppy pot.

7. Slurry the two edges and press together carefully but firmly. Methods of making this joint decorative are indicated below.

8. Stand the base of the pot, still around the tube, onto a slice of clay the same thickness as the walls of the pot. Mark around the base, remove the pot, cut off the surplus clay, slurry the edges where the walls and the base will join, and press the walls and base firmly together.

9. While the tube or block is still inside the pot, decorative strips can be added and impressed decoration can be pressed into the soft clay surface of the pot with pieces of wood, screw heads, bolts and a variety of other interesting objects.

When the pot has firmed-up a little, decoration can be cut into the surface.

10. While the clay is still leather-hard but able to support itself remove the tube or block from inside the newspaper then, by twisting the paper, remove this. If small pieces of paper are left in the pot they will burn away during firing.

It is essential to remove the tube before the clay gets too dry, for the clay will contract and make the removal of the tube difficult. The clay is likely to crack for the same reason.

The pot is now complete except for any surface finishing that may be necessary or required.

Projects using the wrap-around method

1. *Lapped edge pots* A wrap-around pot is made as described except that the vertical edge is not trimmed so that a butt joint can be made (Sections 6 and 7). Instead, the excess width of clay is rolled or pinched so that there is not a bulky overlap.

The two surfaces are then joined with slurry, the overlap forming a decorative line, or it can be pressed in with the end of the finger or with a decorative stamp. Decorative bands can also be

applied around the pot with decorative over-lapping edges.

2. *Jars with lids* Wrap-around pots can be made into useful jars for storing jam, herbs, tea, even spaghetti. The proposed contents will determine the size of jar required, remembering that the pot will be about one-tenth smaller when completed and fired than it was when made.

The body of the jar is made as described for a basic wrap-around pot. The lid can be flat if it is to be under 8 cm (3 in) in diameter. If it is to be over this width it is advisable to dome it over or in a dish mould so as to avoid sagging in the glaze firing.

A coil or strip of clay is joined on the underside of the lid so as to form a flange that will keep the lid in place. A knob or handle is then joined to the top of the lid if this is desired.

Sets of jars can be made in this way and the name or a symbol for the contents can be applied to or carved in the wall of the jar.

3. *Tube sculpture* Wrap-around pots can be joined together in many ways to make interesting sculptural groups. One method is to make a group of five or more narrow pots of differing heights. They can either be given individual bases or they can be joined to one common base. The tops can be pinched so that they splay out rather like a simple sea creature such as a sea-anemone. The group of tubes is then joined together with slurry and carefully finished.

Tube pots with thin, pinched edges can be ideal when using porcelain, for the thin edges become translucent.

4. *Lamp bases* If a reasonably stable wrap-around pot is made a narrow neck can either be slab built or coiled to accommodate a light fitting. The opening needs to be about 2 cm ($\frac{3}{4}$ in) in diameter when damp. A 6 mm ($\frac{1}{4}$ in) hole should be made near the base for the electric flex to pass through. Lamp bases are discussed more fully in the sections on coil and slab pots.

5. *Shallow dishes* Shallow dishes, large and small, can be made by wrapping a narrow strip of clay around a tube of suitable diameter. The method is the same as for a basic wrap-around pot.

6. *Figures* Humorous and interesting

figures can be made by using a number of wrap-around tubes for the body, head and limbs. The various sections should be made and allowed to become leather-hard before joining them together. Coils and modelled sections can be added to give the figure character, suggest clothing and to decorate. Pots using two narrow tubes joined to one larger tube, rather like the legs and truncated body of a man or woman, can be useful as well as interesting objects.

There are many other figures which the keen and adventurous student can create based on simple wrap-around forms.

7. *Winged pots* Instead of wrapping one slice of clay around a tube two slices can be used to make a wide, slim pot with a tubular opening in the centre. Newspaper is wrapped around a suitable tube as described for a basic wrap-around pot. Two slices of clay are cut, the edges of which can be straight and of even thickness, or rolled and pinched to make them thin. The slices are then put together with the tube separating them in the middle. The edges of the slices are then pinched together as in Fig. 10B.

Fig. 10. Winged pots

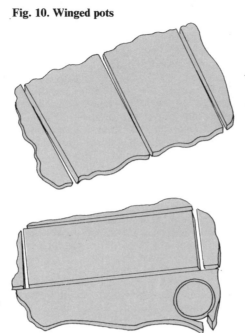

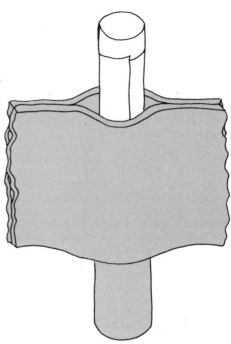

10A: The clay cut ready for assembly, with two slices to make the 'wings', one slice to make a cylindrical stand, and a circular base.

10B: The 'wings' placed around a tube wrapped with newspaper. The two slices have been pinched together at their edges.

10C: Looking onto the assembled pot, showing how the cylindrical base supports the 'wings'.

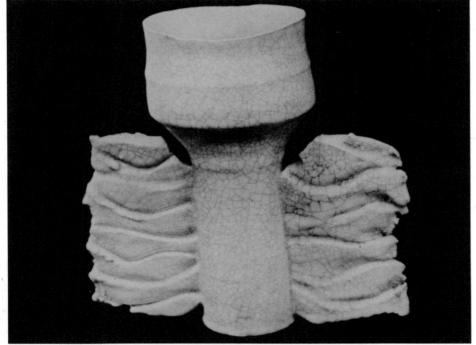

Plate 16. Porcelain wing pot by Colin Pearson, owned by R. Fielden.

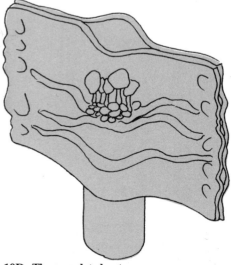

10D: The completed pot.

35

SLAB POTS AND OTHER PROJECTS

The pinching dents can be effective as decoration. The joined slices can either be joined to a flat base or raised up on a cylindrical tube. This type of pot can be an excellent project for there is much scope for experiment and variation. The flat sides can be decorated in a number of ways such as by carving, the addition of relief and brushed slip.

Press moulding

Moulded pots, particularly shallow dishes, are great favourites among part-time student potters. The moulds are normally not made by the students using them, they are merely a means of churning out objects for Christmas presents. They require virtually no craftsmanship and no creative ability. In addition, plaster moulds can be a hazard, for if plaster gets into the clay it can cause flaking after firing. I think these comments indicate my general dislike for moulded dishes and I would advise any teacher who intends that his students should achieve a reasonable standard of craftsmanship to either forbid or strongly discourage the making of such pressed items. It is surely quite reasonable to claim that pottery classes are run so that the students can experience the pleasure of using clay, acquire a standard of craftsmanship

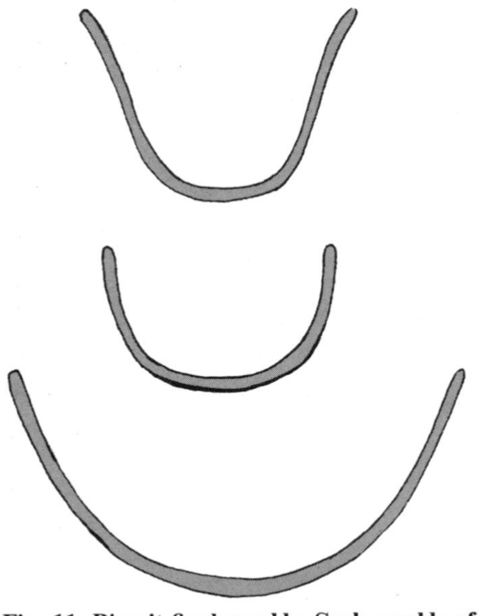

Fig. 11. Biscuit-fired moulds. Such moulds of varying size and shape are useful for making composite pots.

36

and in so doing make pots, some of which will be fired and taken home. I can see little point in running classes so that badly-made pots requiring little or no thought can be made for Christmas presents.

Despite this general criticism, press moulds *can* be very useful when making spherical bottles and some types of dish. It is useful to have a selection of biscuit-fired moulds hemi-spherical in shape and of varying diameters. Such moulds are soon thrown by the teacher and can be used for pressing clay in or over. They are seldom of use for mass producing Christmas presents! Biscuit moulds are better than plaster moulds if many students are to use them due to the danger of plaster chips getting into the clay.

Suitable clays

Most clays are suitable for use in or over a mould. If the moulded section is but part of a pot the same clay should be used for all sections of the pot.

Method of Making

For a sphere

1. Cut or roll out a slice of well-prepared soft clay large enough to go in or over the mould. It is easier to coax the clay over a mould, but great care must be taken to separate the clay from the mould before the clay contracts and consequently cracks. It is more difficult to coax the clay inside the mould without the clay pleating, but the danger of the clay cracking is negligible. Only practice will indicate the best method for each student.
2. Having placed the clay in or over the mould, trim off any surplus clay with a knife or wire.
3. If two identical moulds are available the second hemisphere can be made; if not, the first hemisphere should be removed when it is just firm enough to support itself and a second hemisphere made in the same mould. The first hemisphere should be kept damp by wrapping it in plastic.
4. When both hemispheres are made and able to support themselves without sagging, yet still damp, thicken the rims by tapping down gently with a flat stick.
5. Apply slurry to the rims and place the two rims together. Press the two sections together.
6. Use a piece of hack-saw blade to weld the two sections together.

7. The completed sphere can now be beaten into shape with a flat stick. The air-tight sphere is remarkably strong and can be finished to any shape based on a sphere. Dents can be impressed, feet added, coiled necks added and when it is leather-hard, holes can be cut into it.

The same press moulds can be used for making pots based on a bowl form, spherical form or any part thereof. Strips of clay can be placed over the mould and joined together so that the resulting joins form the decoration. The moulds are also useful when doming lids and curving slabs before their assembly.

Another use is to build a pot by pressing pellets, coils and slices onto the inside of the mould. The various sections need to overlap or be joined together by scraping one section into the next with a modelling tool. The pattern formed by the various sections will remain on the outside of the pot provided the sections are not pressed down too hard. Building can continue beyond the mould so that the mould acts as a support as well as a former, for a larger pot.

Box Pots

Cardboard boxes make excellent moulds for pots made with pellets, coils and strips.

When all the pieces have been placed inside, including the base, and these have been welded together, the box should be cut and torn away from the clay. An Inca wall is revealed! If the clay is allowed to dry the removal of the box will break the pot.

Such box pots can make an excellent project and assuming that they have been put together with some care, the results will be pleasing.

Combining hand-building methods

The hand-building methods that have been described do not have to be used exclusively. They can be combined and adapted in numerous ways. Some ways in which methods can be combined have already been mentioned, such as the coiling of a narrow neck onto a slab bottle.

It is better to master each method before combining them, but once mastered it is possible to make an almost limitless range of forms by combining methods.

THE POTTER'S WHEEL

The potter's wheel was probably first used in the Near East. It was used in Egypt from the commencement of recorded history and its use probably spread from this area to China and Europe before 2000 B.C. Whereas hand-building was, and to a large extent continues to be, the work of women, the wheel seems to have been the prerogative of men.

The basic principle of the wheel is of a flat wheel-head made of wood or metal which revolves with considerable momentum. The momentum is ensured by having a heavy wheel-head or more commonly, a fly-wheel. The means of propulsion can be hand, foot or motor and there must be a means of controlling the speed smoothly without any jolting.

Hand wheels

The hand-wheel is now peculiar to China and Japan. It has a heavy wooden head into which four notches are cut near the circumference. The wheel-head is placed over a shaft which is firmly fixed into the ground or a slab of stone (See Fig. 12). A stick is inserted into one of the notches and turned vigorously. The stick is removed and the momentum of the wheel lasts long enough to make a small pot. The momentum requires constant renewal if a larger pot is to be made.

This method might appear to be laborious yet Bernard Leach comments that the day's output of an Oriental thrower using such a wheel, compares favourably with that of a Western potter using a crank driven kick-wheel.

Shoji Hamada, the famous Japanese potter, continues to use a hand-driven wheel although he is well-acquainted with the kick and power driven wheels of the West. The method of making a pot, including the type of wheel used, very much influences the form and 'feel' of a pot. The same basic pot made by a potter on a kick wheel and then an electrically powered wheel will only be superficially the same, for on examination they will be found to have a very different presence and 'feel'.

Kick wheels

In the West we use two main types of kick wheel; one is frequently called a continental wheel, the other a cranked or Leach wheel. The continental wheel has a large dome-topped fly wheel running on a straight shaft. A wheel head is fixed to the top of the shaft, the wheel-head being level with a seat for the potter. There is no tray to catch the slurry.

The cranked wheel has a fly-wheel placed at the base of the vertical shaft; above this the shaft is cranked. The crank is connected by a block to a kick bar. It is important that the proportions of the crank and bar allow an easy long kick so as to avoid jerking the body. The wheel head is at the top of the shaft and approximately 20 cm (8 in) above the seat for the potter. With most wheels, a

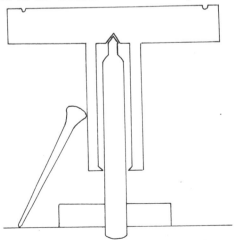

Fig. 12. Handwheel used in Japan. The heavy wooden wheel-head revolves on a shaft firmly fixed into the ground. The wheel is rotated with a stick inserted into a notch in the wheel head.

CHAPTER 6

tray about 20 cm (8 in) deep is built around the wheel head to contain slurry, water and trimmings.

Power-driven wheels

There have been and still are many types of power-driven wheels. They range from a 'slave' wheel which was turned by an apprentice for his master to the modern electric wheels with transistorized speed control. The scope of this book does not permit a detailed description of such wheels but cheap, untried electric wheels are seldom worth using or buying. They frequently slow down when centring the clay and they seldom have adequate speed control. To be recommended is the well-tried but expensive electric wheels in which the speed is governed by the friction of two cones placed head to tail so that by altering the angle of one changes the point of contact and therefore the speed of the other. Another satisfactory but cheaper electric wheel is that driven by a D.C. motor with electronic speed control. These are now marketed by most potters' merchants under different names, with varying finishes and at greatly varying prices.

The cone-driven wheels have the advantage of being very robust with little to go wrong but they are not very sensitive to speed variation, particularly if very slow speeds are required for wide pots.

The wheels with D.C. motors and electronic speed control have the advantage of excellent speed variation even at very low speeds but there is a more intricate mechanism to go wrong which will, in such an event, require the services of a skilled electrician. Whichever wheel is used the basic principles of making are the same.

Historical background to throwing

This subject is vast since the majority of pots made by man since before 2000 B.C. have been made on the wheel. This includes the early Chinese pots of the Han dynasty (206 B.C.–A.D. 220) to the present day and the majority of European pots, from the Greeks and Romans to the industrial revolution of the late 18th century when mass-produced moulded pots started to ease the thrower from his dominant position until, in the 1930's there were very few throwers left.

Thanks to the work and writings of Bernard Leach and others, thrown pottery is enjoying a remarkable revival. The reasons are somewhat mixed. On the one hand it has been proved that the thrown functional pot compares favourably with the better mass-produced product in price, usefulness and appearance. On the other hand modern house interiors, which have become rather severe and hard-lined, seem to need something earthy, warm, even rough as a contrast. Stoneware pottery and sculptural forms seem to satisfy such a need.

An outline of the development of pottery from early times to the present day appears in Chapter 13.

Suitable Clays

Particular care must be taken when selecting and preparing clay for throwing. Unless this is done it is quite useless struggling to centre the clay and make a pot. More students fail and become disillusioned about throwing because the clay was not properly prepared than for any other single reason. I have seen students push a few odds and ends of clay into a ball shape, slam it onto the wheel and then cry for help because they cannot centre the clay, let alone make a pot. An experienced potter can only help in such a situation by advising that he would always prepare his clay thoroughly and never attempt to throw a pot from odd scraps of clay.

The clay selected should be plastic, soft and free of coarse grog. Some clays, such as a fine earthenware body, can be somewhat slimy and waxy in which case the addition of sand or a fine grog would be an advantage. If large pots, 5 kg (11 lbs), are to be made—and this will only be by a competent thrower—it is advisable to knead in some additional grog as this will give the pot extra strength during the throwing process and reduce the shrinkage rate and consequently the risk of cracking.

Sufficient clay should be kneaded for the throwing session, whether it be a couple of hours or a day. This will save time and prevent repeated interruptions of the throwing process. Until the clay is kneaded competently it is quite useless attempting to throw with it. This fact, sad though it may be, cannot be over emphasised.

The consistency of the clay is also important. A simple test is to press the thumb into the clay. If it presses in with ease yet leaves a clean imprint the clay is probably right for throwing. If it was too soft to knead it will be too soft to throw, but if it was just a little sticky when kneading it is probably right for throwing. Practice and first-hand advice from a competent potter are the only fool-proof ways of finding out!

When the clay is ready, use a wire to cut lumps of a suitable size. Always weigh up clay of a given weight and note the weight and size of the pot made. Never use a random weight and hope for the best, for it is only by knowing that a certain weight of clay will yield a pot of a given approximate size that the clay will be used to the full and not left as a heavy wall near the base of the pot. See the accompanying table as a guide.

The following chart indicates the size of article that can normally be thrown from a given weight of clay. Always weigh up clay before throwing commences; it is the only way to throw efficiently and uniformly.

Item	Weight	Height	Width	Item	Weight	Height	Width
Basic cylinder	500 gms (1 lb 2 oz)	130 mm (3 in)	90 mm (5 in)	Dinner plates	1.800 kg (4 lb) Turned foot	38 mm (1½ in)	280 mm (11 in)
Small bowl, cereals, etc.	500 gms (1 lb 2 oz) No turning	80 mm (5 in)	130 mm (3½ in)	Casseroles large flat	2.000 kg (4 lbs 8 oz) No turning	100 mm (4 in)	At opening 240 mm (9½ in)
Medium bowl for salads, fruit etc.	1.500 kg (3 lbs 6 oz) To be turned	100 mm (4 in)	200 mm (8 in)	Lid	1.500 kg (3 lbs 6 oz) Turned. Extra clay for knob	38 mm (1½ in)	240 mm (9½ in)
Large bowl	4.00 kg (9 lbs) To be turned	130 mm (5 in)	270 mm (10½ in)	Casserole Medium size	3.000 kg (6 lbs 12 oz) No Turning	180 mm (7 in)	At opening 200 mm (8 in)
Coffee mugs	350 gms (12 oz) No turning	115 mm (4½ in)	83 mm (3¼ in)	Lid	1.000 kg (2 lbs 4 oz) Turned. Extra clay for knob	38 mm (1½ in)	200 mm (8 in)
Tea cups	320 gms (11 oz) Turned foot	90 mm (3½ in)	90 mm (3½ in)	Tea pot 2 cup size	400 gms (14 oz) No turning. Lid opening approx 50 mm (2 in)	90 mm (3½ in)	100 mm (4 in)
Saucers	450 gms (1 lb) Turned foot	18 mm (¾ in)	170 mm (6½ in)	Lid	100 gms (4 oz)		50 mm (2 in)
Store jar	500 gms (1 lb 2 oz) No turning	130 mm (5 in)	at opening 100 mm (4 in)	Tea pot 4 cup size	700 gms (1 lb 9 oz) No turning. Lid opening approx 60 mm (2¼ in)	115 mm (4½ in)	130 mm (5 in)
Lid for store jar	160 gms (6½ oz) Turned. Extra clay for knob		100 mm (4 in)	Lid	200 gms (8 oz)		60 mm (2¼ in)

THE POTTER'S WHEEL

A suitable weight for the beginner is 500 gms (1 lb 2 oz). This is just large enough so as not to be too fiddling, yet it is easily managed without great physical effort. By holding the clay in the hands and banging the corners make the clay into a sphere.

Before outlining the method by which pots can be thrown here is a list of the other processes that may be involved in making and completing thrown pots. Once a few pots have been made the order will seem quite obvious but for a beginner it may be a little confusing.

1. Prepare clay.
2. Throw pots.
3. Throw lids.
4. Turn pots and lids when leather-hard.
5. Apply handles while pot is still leather-hard.
6. Slip decorate or incise if this is desired, while leather-hard.
7. Dry and fire the pots.

Method

The method described here is not the only method, it is just an attempt to put into words one approach to what is essentially a practical task. As with all crafts, considerable practice is essential. This does not mean a few hours but many hours, even years of intensive practice.

So all beginners should take heart if they are not proficient throwers after a few attempts. Likewise, those who have become proficient, but grit their teeth with anxiety as they throw, can look forward to a time when a new feeling of confidence and ease becomes apparent!

Many of the problems experienced by the beginner can be traced to two main causes. The first is lack of practice and the consequent inability to be at one with the clay, feeling its behaviour at all times. The second cause is frequently over-ambitious projects, both in size and form. Until a ball of clay weighing about 500 gms (1 lb) can be centred and pulled up into a straight-sided cylinder it is quite pointless to do battle with a 5 kg (11 lb) lump or to attempt making tea pots!

To summarise, much practice is necessary, and you must master one stage at a time. The fluidity and beauty of a thrown form will only come when the throwing processes are fully mastered and require little apparent effort.

So here is an outline method for making a cylinder 130 mm (5 in) high and 90 mm (3½ in) diameter from 500 gms (1 lb 2 oz) of clay.

1. Throw the clay into the centre of a barely damp wheel head. If the wheel-head or the clay ball is wet the clay will not stick to the wheel.
2. Rotate the wheel at a fairly rapid rate. If it is a kick wheel go as fast as is possible without the body moving. With practice the leg will kick and vary the speed without conscious effort. The wheel should rotate in an anti-clockwise direction.
3. Wet the hands so that they are lubricated. This should be repeated whenever the hands start to stick to the clay.
4. Place the right hand around the clay, then the left hand. The hands must be kept absolutely steady, even though the clay will try to make them move. This is helped if the elbows are pressed into the waist and the arms rested on the tray of the wheel.
5. The clay is then squeezed with the right hand and the heel of the left hand so that it rises into a cone.
6. Release the hands smoothly, without a jerk, so that the cone is not knocked off centre. It is essential that the hands are always released without a jerk, otherwise the pot will be put off-centre.
7. The palm of the right hand is then pressed down onto the top of the cone, the left hand steadying the right hand.
8. The process of pushing the clay into a cone then back into a flattened ball shape is repeated four or five times. The process is called balling and coning, and as well as centring the clay it helps to get it in a mobile condition for subsequent throwing.
9. With both hands around the clay and the right thumb across the clay, apply an even pressure, keeping the hands perfectly still. On releasing the pressure smoothly the clay should be centred.

If it is not centred repeat processes 1–9; this may require much practice.
10. When the clay has been centred press the first two fingers of the right hand into the centre of the clay. Press down until about 7 mm (¼ in) of clay is left at the base.
11. Pull the fingers towards the body,

Fig. 13. Throwing

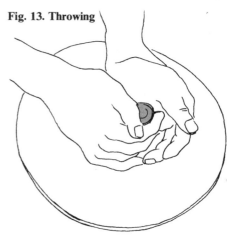

13A: Centring the clay and squeezing it into a cone. The right hand is inside the left hand as the wheel rotates anti-clockwise. *Stage 5*

13B: Centring the clay. Both hands are used to centre the clay. The right thumb ensures a slightly domed top. The left hand has been lifted to show the position of the right thumb. *Stage 9*

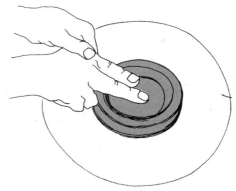

13C: Opening out the clay. The fingers of the right hand press down and are then pulled towards the body. *Stages 10 and 11*

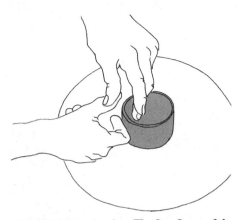

13D: Pulling up the clay. The first finger of the right hand is crooked against the outside and the fingers of the left hand oppose its pressure from the inside. Note: Whenever possible have the hands in contact with each other as this helps them work together. *Stages 12 and 13*

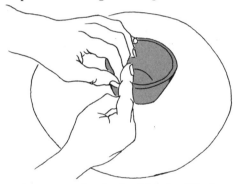

13E: Compressing the rim. This should be done after each pull-up to keep the rim firm and prevent splitting. *Stage 14*

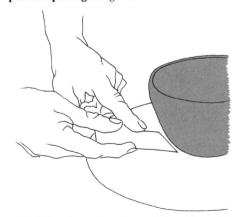

13F: Trimming with a tapered piece of wood to remove slurry and to undercut the pot at an angle of 45°. *Stage 17*

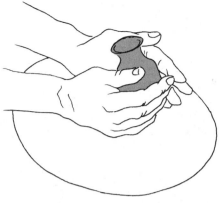

13G: Lifting a cylindrical pot from the wheel, using the flat palms of both hands. *Stage 20*

making a flat base 6–8 cm (2½–3 in) wide.

12. With the fingers of the left hand inside the pot and the first finger of the right hand crooked against the outside, the clay is squeezed and lifted. Always work on the right of the pot.

13. Repeat the pulling-up process, 12, always squeezing the clay harder at the base and gradually releasing the pressure as the hands move up the pot.

14. After each pull-up hold the rim between the thumb and first finger of the left hand and compress the rim with the first finger of the right hand. This will keep the rim firm, prevent it from becoming too thin, and so prevent it from splitting. As the pot increases in size reduce the speed of the wheel.

15. Always aim to make a narrower pot than is actually required. For example when making a cylinder direct the hands when pulling up, towards the centre, as though a conical shape was intended. This is to compensate for the centrifugal force which makes the pot splay out.

16. When the wall of the pot is an even thickness, in this case about 7 mm (¼ in), give it its final shape. Shaping is achieved by gently squeezing the clay and at the same time varying the position of the right hand as compared to the left hand. Experience will show just how to position the hands for the required shape.

17. When the throwing and shaping have been completed the base of the wall should be trimmed with a tapered piece of bamboo or a piece of ruler cut at an angle of 45°. The tool should be held firmly and used to remove any surplus clay at the base of the pot wall and to undercut it at an angle of 45°.

Some of the slurry on the wall of the pot should also be removed by holding the tool against the wall of the pot, while supporting it from the inside with the left hand.

18. Use a soft sponge to remove any water from inside the pot. The pot should be rotating, not stationary, so as to avoid distortion.

19. Holding the cutting wire taut and hard down onto the top of the wheel head, pull it under the pot. This may be done with the wheel stationary or slowly rotating. The latter probably loosens the pot better and gives the shell-like pattern which is characteristic of the pots made at the Leach pottery.

20. Lift the pot from the wheel to a clean board, using the flat palms of both hands, which should be free of slurry. The lifting action should be a peeling motion as opposed to a straight, vertical lift. Always take care when lifting and placing down a newly-thrown pot, but do not be timid.

Some amateur potters slide their pots from the wheel using considerable quantities of water. This method probably requires less initial courage but it tends to distort the pot more and it takes rather longer. Take courage and lift the pot!

21. If the pots need turning or skimming they should be put aside until they are leather-hard. If they are complete they should be left to dry. When the making of a small cylinder has been mastered—when ten or more cylinders of the same size can be made with some fluency, and not before—larger cylinders using more clay can be made and other shapes embarked upon.

The method of making larger cylinders is the same as described for a small cylinder except that the larger the pot, particularly in diameter, the slower the wheel must rotate. That does not mean that the wheel should only creep around, for it should only rotate very slowly for plates and bowls of 45 cm (18 in) plus diameter.

Collaring

This is the term applied to the squeezing in and narrowing of a pot. It is useful when a proposed cylinder starts to

THE POTTER'S WHEEL

flare out at the rim and for all narrow necked pots, such as pitchers, bottles, flasks, spheres and teapot spouts. It tends to thicken the wall of the pot, for a given amount of clay is being compressed into a wall of reduced circumference. Unless care is taken the clay has a tendency to buckle or pleat.

The basic rules for collaring are:

1. *Increase the speed of the wheel as the pot is reduced in diameter.*
2. *Do not expect to narrow the pot in one brief operation.*
3. *Place both hands around the pot, in a strangling position, and gently squeeze the pot, moving the hands up the pot as the diameter is reduced.*
4. *After each reduction in the diameter, and certainly if there is any tendency of the clay to buckle, pull up the wall of the pot in the same way as for throwing.*
5. *Use as little water as possible.*
6. *Repeat the process until the required diameter and shape are obtained.*

Bowls

A bowl is made in a similar way to that described for a cylinder. The main difference is in the initial opening out of the centred clay. This is for two reasons; a bowl rarely requires a flat base inside, it needs to be a continuous, flowing curve with little or no change in direction. Secondly, a bowl frequently needs to have a foot ring so that the curving form springs up from it. A bowl can be dumpy and graceless, whereas it should be full of life, and vigour, springing up from the table.

Shoji Hamada, speaking of his approach to pottery has said:

Fig. 14. Section of a bowl showing how it springs up from the foot ring.

42

Plate 18. The workshop of Shoji Hamada's pottery in Masheko, Japan.

'*I would like to see the day when all that I make can be at least declared not bad. Standing in the vegetable garden gives me a feeling of utter defeat, everything growing naturally, and splendidly, not in the least concerned with me or my eyes! If only pots too could be thus born and not made. If only pots—the rims of bowls and lips of bottles could have the appearance of being in mid-growth, in motion, for ever unsuspended!*

'*It has always been said that the best tea bowls look larger inside than on the outside. I feel this saying expresses the very essence of pottery making.*'

Quote from Hamada Shoji Introduction by Yanagi and B. Leach Asahi Shimbun Publishing Co.

The basic rules for making a bowl are:

1. *When making the initial opening in the centred clay (Fig. 14) leave the base thick enough so as to turn a foot-ring if this is so desired.*
2. *When enlarging the initial opening be sure to allow the fingers of the right hand to rise, so that a curved base is made and not a flat base.*
3. *When pulling up the walls of the bowl take care not to press down with the left hand otherwise the curving base will not flow into the wall of the bowl.*
4. *Finish the rim with a piece of soft leather (see Fig. 15A). This will compress the rim and give it a smooth finish. With*

Fig. 15. Making a bowl

15A: Finishing the rim with a strip of soft leather. *Stage 4*

15B: Lifting a bowl from the wheel, using splayed fingers. *Stage 6*

the exception of porcelain, it is probably better to make the rims of bowls and most functional pots marginally thicker than the walls. This will give the pots physical and visual strength.

5. Using the tapered bamboo tool, trim off as much surplus clay at the base as is possible without causing the bowl to collapse from lack of support. This will make turning much easier.

6. Cut and lift the bowl onto a clean board. It might prove easier to use splayed out fingers instead of the flat palms for lifting (see Fig. 15B).

Spheres

The main problems that are likely to be experienced when throwing spheres are that they will be thick and heavy, particularly near the base and they have a tendency to collapse if an attempt is made to throw them thinly.

Turning the base at the leather-hard stage is a little more involved than it is for bowls and cylindrical forms because the sphere cannot be inverted on the wheel without the danger of collapsing it. To overcome this problem a chuck, which will accommodate the sphere, is thrown and allowed to firm-up but not dry. See below.

The basic rules for throwing a sphere are:

1. Centre and open out as for a bowl. Make the inside curve of the base such that it will flow into the curved wall of the sphere.

2. Pull up the clay as for a cylinder but do not make it too thin, allowing for thinning when it is pushed out into a sphere.

3. Use as little water as possible so that the clay does not become too soft and more liable to collapse.

4. When all the clay has been thrown into the cylinder, expand the wall a little at a time from the inside until the sphere is complete.

5. If necessary the opening can be reduced by collaring.

6. Remove any water from inside the pot. If the opening is narrow tie a sponge to the end of a thin stick or cane.

7. Remove slurry and excess clay from the base of the pot and lift it onto a clean board.

Making a chuck

A chuck is necessary whenever a pot needs support in addition to that given by the rim. A sphere comes into this category. The chuck should be made from the same clay as the pot and it should be made sometime before the pots are to be turned so that it firms-up and is not sticky. The procedure for making a chuck is as follows:

1. Prepare the clay as for throwing and cut off a lump of adequate size.

2. Centre the clay.

3. Open out as for throwing a sphere, making the curve such that the sphere will rest in it.

4. If the sphere is large pull up the wall of the chuck a little, keeping it thick, about 15 mm ($\frac{1}{2}$ in). Check that the chuck will accommodate the sphere.

5. Leave the chuck to firm-up.

6. When the pot is ready for turning it should be placed in the chuck and centred.

Due to the time involved in making a chuck it is advantageous to have a number of pots that are the same or that can at least use the same chuck.

Lids and galleries

Pots and bowls with lids should not be attempted until pots of a given size can be made with some certainty and fluency. A badly-fitting lid can be the cause of annoyance, if it is too large for the opening it is quite useless. A lid that fits well can give satisfaction to the user and is evidence of competent craftsmanship.

The lid should always be considered when designing a pot so that it is part of the overall form and not an intrusive 'hat'. The design of the lid is to a large extent dictated by the means used to keep it in position. For some pots it is essential that the lid stays in position even when the pot is tilted over; for others, such as store jars, a wide opening is desirable.

Six of the most common lids and the galleries, where necessary, are illustrated in Fig. 16. Some, such as illustration E which is frequently used for teapots, are quite complicated, requiring a gallery and a lid with a flange. Before the lidded pot is started the type of lid should be decided upon. This will depend on the function, shape and size of the pot. If it is to be a teapot types B, D and E only are suitable if the lid is to remain in position while the pot is tilted. For a casserole, type C and F are probably the most satisfactory. If

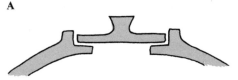

A

Fig. 16. Lid fittings
The diagrams illustrate six of the most common lid fittings. Types A, C, E and F require a gallery to be made when making the pot. Types A and B are the simplest lids to make as, unlike the other lids, they do not require turning. Care must be taken to choose a lid type most suited to the form and function of the pot.

B

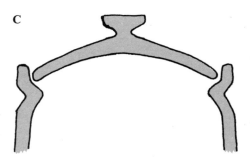

C

D

E

F

Fig. 17. Making a gallery for a teapot. Such a gallery is necessary for lids type A, C and E.

the pot is wide, 15 cm (6 in) plus flat lids such as A and B could warp in a stoneware firing if, as is the usual practice, they are fired in the pot.

Lids should always be made from the same clay as the pot and all measurements taken when the pot is wet after throwing, either with callipers or a notched ruler, allowing between 2 mm and 6 mm ($\frac{1}{16}$ in and $\frac{1}{4}$ in) play, for it is useless having a lid that is too big. Some allowance must also be given for the pot not being perfectly circular.

It is much better to make a series of pots with the same opening measurement, then the lids for them; rather than a pot then a lid, then a pot and so on.

If the pot requires a gallery as in types A and E, the wall of the pot should be pulled up part way, keeping the rim thick. The rim is then split in half by pressing down with the first finger. See Fig. 17. The gallery should be generous and fairly thick so that it accommodates the lid with ease and so that it is not easily chipped.

The throwing of the pot can now be completed, if necessary tidying up the gallery when throwing has been completed.

Basic method for lid type A
1. Prepare and weigh up the clay. For a store jar lid try 200 gms (8 oz) and adjust the weight as necessary.
2. Centre the clay and make the flattened ball approximately the width of the lid opening.
3. Isolate a knob and check the width of the lid with the callipers. The lid is now

complete except for finishing the edge with a soft leather, cutting and lifting-off. It can be lifted by the knob if a thin metal scraper is used to release the suction of the lid to the wheel-head.

Basic method for lid type B
This lid is particularly useful for store jars and for teapots. If the lid is small, 6 cm (2$\frac{1}{2}$ in) diameter and less, it is sometimes better to make the lid without a knob for the lid can be lifted by its rim and the knob can in some cases make the lid and pot appear cluttered.
1. Prepare and weigh up the clay.
2. Centre the clay and make the flattened ball approximately the width of the lid opening.
3. Isolate the knob if a knob is required or open out the clay into a shallow dish. This will form a small collar around the circumference.
4. Throw a cylinder about 4 cm (1$\frac{1}{2}$ in) high from the collar formed at stage 3. The diameter of the cylinder should be just less than the opening into which the lid will fit.
5. Using a piece of ruler cut at 45°, remove the slurry and ensure the accuracy of the cylinder thrown in stage 4.
6. Under-cut the base at an angle of 45°.
7. Fold the top 13 mm–20 mm ($\frac{1}{2}$ in–$\frac{3}{4}$ in) of the cylinder outwards, so forming a horizontal flange. The flange may be folded over even further if this would make the lid fit more snugly on the pot opening.
8. Use a leather to finish the flange.
9. Cut off the lid with a wire and lift it onto a clean board.

The lid is now complete and assuming all measurements were correct, it will not need to be turned. If turning is necessary a small chuck will be required to protect the knob.

Basic method for type C
1. Prepare and weigh up the clay.
2. Throw a shallow dish just less than the pot opening.
3. Finish the rim with a leather.
4. Under-cut at 45°, cut off with a wire and lift the lid onto a clean board.
5. When the lid is leather-hard and ready for turning, place it centrally on the wheel with a clay blob under the centre to prevent any distortion during turning.
6. Turn off all surplus clay so that the lid is of even thickness; the inside and outside curves being the same.

Fig. 18. Lid type B

18A: The clay centred and approximately the diameter of the proposed lid. *Stage 2*

18B: The knob isolated and shaped. *Stage 3*

18C: A cylinder must be of the required diameter to fit the pot opening. *Stage 4*

18D: All slurry removed and the cylinder undercut at 45°. *Stages 5 and 6*

18E: The top of the cylinder folded over to form a flange. *Stage 7*

7. Cross-hatch and paint with slurry, the centre of the lid ready to accept the clay for the knob.
8. Take a small ball of clay, of the same type as that used to throw the lid and pot, and press it firmly onto the lid. Weld the edges of the ball into the lid.
9. Using as little water as possible, centre the clay ball and shape the knob.
10. Remove any surplus slurry and lift the lid from the wheel.

It is essential that the lid is supported in the centre during turning and the throwing of the knob. If this is not done the lid will splay out and become too large. This is particularly true with large lids for casseroles.

Basic method for type D

This type of lid should only be used for small pots so that they can be lifted easily without the aid of a knob. They are excellent for jars and teapots. The pot must have a shoulder and a vertical collar.

1. Prepare and weigh up the clay.
2. Throw a shallow bowl the depth of the pot's collar. The base should be gently curved, not flat, and the sides vertical. The diameter should be the same as the collar, allowing a little free play, 3 mm ($\frac{1}{8}$ in).
3. Under-cut, cut off with a wire and lift onto a clean board.
4. When leather-hard, place the lid on a clay pad with a supporting blob of clay under the centre. The pad will protect the rim of the lid.
5. Turn off any surplus clay so that the lid is of even thickness and the inside and outside curves are sympathetic.
6. Carefully lift from the pad. The lid is complete.

Basic method for type E

This type of lid is excellent for teapots for it has little tendency to fall out, even when the pot is tipped at 90°. It is also good when the line of the pot is required to continue through into the lid, as opposed to the more articulated lines of most other types of lid.

The pot must be thrown with a gallery, ready to accept the lid.

1. Prepare and weigh up the clay. This type of lid requires rather more clay than those so far described, for it has two flanges and will require turning.
2. Centre the clay and open out into a shallow bowl with a substantial collar of

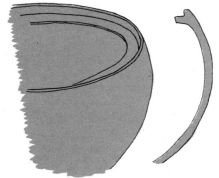

Fig. 19. A gallery on a casserole, showing a section of the pot. Lid type C is suitable for casseroles.

clay around the circumference, 13 mm– 20 mm ($\frac{1}{2}$ in–$\frac{3}{4}$ in) wide.

3. Divide the collar into two, using the nail of the thumb or first finger.
4. Squeeze the outer half of the collar to form the horizontal flange. Check by measuring that it will fit onto the gallery of the pot with a minimum of free play.
5. Throw the remaining collar into a vertical flange that will be high enough to cause the lid to wedge in the opening when the pot is tilted for pouring. Check the width of the flange ensuring that it will sit on the gallery with a minimum of free play.
6. Under-cut, cut off with a wire and lift onto a clean board.
7. When leather-hard the top of the lid must be turned. This can be done on a pad of clay thrown on the wheel head, or by using the pot, to which the lid will belong, as a chuck. The second method is better if the line of the pot is to continue through into the lid. The pot must also be leather-hard, like the lid. Turn off all surplus clay, but do not make the horizontal flange too thin as this will encourage chipping and breakage.
8. Cross-hatch and apply slurry to the centre of the lid. Apply a blob of soft clay, centre and make a suitable knob.

The lid is now complete, but ensure that it is eased off the pot and not left firmly fixed to it.

Basic method for lid type F

This type of lid is the same as type E but the pot does not have a gallery. Instead the walls come up almost vertically with no interior obstruction. Such a lid-fitting is ideal when a wide opening is required for storage jars and when a casserole is required without a gallery. Such a casserole can also be used as a bowl.

The method of making this type of lid is exactly the same as described for type E.

Making spouts for teapots and coffee pots

The function of the spout is to allow liquid to be poured from a lidded vessel in a continuous smooth flow and to cut the flow cleanly without any dripping.

To make a spout that functions in this way is not always easy, particularly as the spout, when joined to the body

Fig. 20. Lid types E and F

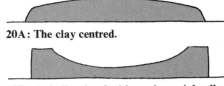

20A: The clay centred.

20B: A shallow bowl with a substantial collar. Stage 2

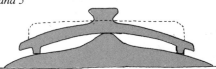

20C: The collar divided into two to form a vertical and a horizontal flange. Stages 3, 4 and 5

20D: The leather-hard lid placed on a pad of clay for turning and the application of a knob. Note the support given by the pad to the centre of the lid. The broken line indicates the shape of the lid prior to turning. Stages 7 and 8

of the pot, must contribute to a unified and satisfying form. A teapot or coffee pot can easily become a collection of unrelated sections; it is important to avoid this and ensure that the sections have unity of form.

To make a spout that will pour well the following factors need to be considered:

1. The base which will join onto the pot must be large so that an adequate grid of holes can be made in the wall of the pot.
2. It must be sufficiently tall to allow the pouring lip to be as high or slightly higher than the gallery. If the top of the spout is lower than the gallery the pot cannot be filled!
3. It must taper continuously to the lip, so that the maximum pressure of liquid is at that point. Trumpet-shaped spouts are unsatisfactory.
4. The inside of the spout should be smooth and free from ridges.
5. The lip should have a good cutting edge to prevent dribbling. This edge should not be so thin and sharp that it is easily chipped.
6. The angle at which the spout is fixed to the body should be as low as possible to aid pouring yet it must not project too

THE POTTER'S WHEEL

far or fail to be as high as the gallery. A compromise is necessary.

Having considered all the above mentioned factors the spout can be thrown. Some potters weigh up clay for each spout, others centre one larger cone of clay from which a dozen or more spouts can be made. I use the second method, finding it easier, particularly for small spouts. It is better to use an electric wheel as higher speeds are necessary.

Basic method for making a spout

1. Prepare and centre clay. If throwing from a cone, isolate enough clay for one spout.
2. Open out a generous base.
3. Pull up a slightly concave cone using the small finger inside as far as possible then a round stick, such as a pencil. The narrower the spout is thrown the faster the wheel must go, particularly if collaring it in.
4. Use a rib to finish the shaping and to remove all the slurry.
5. Under-cut at the base of the spout and cut off, using wire or a needle.
6. The completed spout can either be lifted off and put to dry to the 'soft leather' stage before being attached to the pot or it can be attached straight from the wheel. I prefer the second method but extra care must be taken when handling.
7. Cut the base angle with a wire. Experience will indicate where to cut.
8. Use a wet finger to spread the base

Fig. 21. Spouts

21A: Isolating and opening out a generous base. *Stage 2*

21B: Using a pencil to throw a narrow spout. *Stage 3*

21C: Collaring a spout to reduce its diameter at the top. *Stage 3*

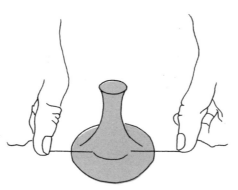

21D: Cutting the base of the spout with a wire prior to application to the pot. *Stage 7*

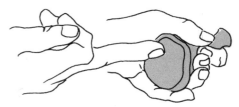

21E: Spreading the base aperture. *Stage 8*

21F: Offering the spout onto the pot and marking its position. *Stage 9*

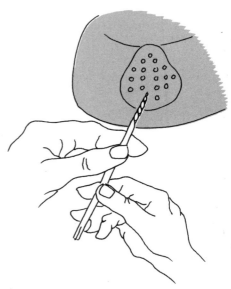

21G: Making the grid of holes using a twist drill. *Stage 10*

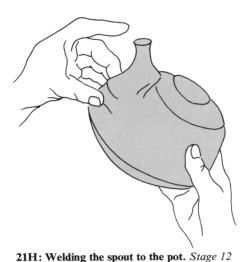

21H: Welding the spout to the pot. *Stage 12*

21I: Trimming the end of the spout with a thin wire. The left hand should be slightly lower than the right. *Stage 13*

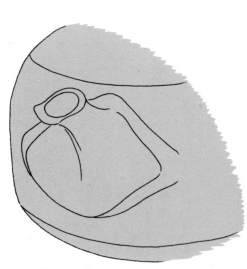

21J: The completed spout.

aperture, particularly that section that will be at the top of the pot.

9. Offer the spout onto the pot so as to check that the base angle is suitable and to make a mark, indicating where the grid of holes is to be made.

10. Using a twist-drill or hole cutter, about 5 mm ($\frac{3}{16}$ in) diameter, make a grid of holes. The holes should be close together and as many as the base area of spout permits to be made.

11. Cross-hatch the pot, where the spout will join it and apply slurry.

12. Weld the spout to the pot. Whether the spout is made to flow from the pot or left rather more articulated is an aesthetic consideration.

13. Trim the end of the spout, either with a thin wire or a sharp knife. Allowance must be made for 'clay memory', that is the tendency for the clay to continue twisting in a clockwise direction during drying and firing. To overcome this difficulty the end of the spout should not be cut horizontally but, facing the end of the spout, the left side should be cut slightly lower than the right.

Knowledge of a particular clay and trials will indicate just how much allowance must be made.

14. When the pot is complete, including a handle or lugs for a cane handle, put it to dry slowly.

15. When dry, rub off any burrs that resulted from drilling the spout grid, from the inside of the pot.

Plate 19. This attractive porcelain teapot is the work of a sixteen-year-old student.

Plate 20. Stoneware coffee pot and mugs.

Plate 21. This stoneware teapot was thrown in sections and then assembled.

THE POTTER'S WHEEL

Handles

A handle is, first and foremost, applied to a pot so that the pot can be lifted and, in many cases, tilted for pouring. This means that matters of function must dictate the width, length and positioning of the handle.

Many early Chinese pots and more recent pots from South America and Africa, have what is considered to be the forerunner of the handle, two pierced lugs, arranged opposite each other. The pot was suspended from these lugs and they acts as pivots when the jug was tilted for pouring.

The handles of some medieval mugs and jugs were made by rolling out a coil, which was partly flattened then firmly attached to the pot.

It was soon learned that by 'pulling' a handle a strap of clay, oval in section, and slightly tapering, could be made to 'flow' from the point of attachment. It is interesting to note that the Japanese potter had not used pulled handles until their introduction by Hamada and Bernard Leach. Before pulling a handle, the size of section and length should be considered. The size of section depends on the size of the pot and the number of fingers that will grasp the handle. A small coffee mug or cup is easily held by one finger and the thumb, a pint tankard will require at least two fingers and the thumb, whilst a half gallon pitcher will need the whole hand. There is little point in making a large handle more than about 5 cm (2 in) wide, for above this size it is difficult to grip.

The length of the handle depends, to a certain extent, on the size and shape of the pot. A pitcher with a concave curve near the rim, resolving into a cylinder near the base, will require a rather larger handle than a pitcher with a more bulbous, convex curve, for the handle has to create the space between it and the body in the first example but the shape of the pitcher creates such a space in the second.

It is essential to have the pots requiring handles in view as the handles are pulled, so that the shape and size can be considered.

Many potters find handle-making difficult. This is probably due to two main causes. More practice is gained with throwing and turning, for most of

Fig. 22. *Handles. Left:* **A pitcher with concave curve near the rim and** (*right*) **a more bulbous pitcher, showing how the shape of the handle takes account of the pot shape.**

a potter's output involves these processes, whereas relatively few items require handles. The second cause is probably lack of suitable clay. The clay must be as well-prepared and barely stiffer than that used for throwing.

I see many students who are otherwise competent potters take a few scraps of clay, push them together and then attempt to pull handles. They wonder why they fail to make good handles!

The basic method for making a pulled handle

1. Prepare clay as for throwing. It may be slightly stiffer than that used for throwing but it should not be too firm as this will result in rather wooden, non-plastic looking handles.

2. Break off a piece of clay that is sufficient to make the handles and leave a substantial lump to grip whilst pulling the handles.

3. Roll and bang the clay into a tapering cylindrical shape.

4. Grip the clay in the left hand at about face level, wet the right hand and begin pulling down sufficient clay for the required handle. Use gentle pressure and quick confident strokes.

5. The pulling motion is repeated, moving the hand around the clay so as to get an oval section and the required width. Wet the hand as the clay becomes sticky. The handle should taper slightly but not become flimsy near the end.

6. The handle should not be pulled to its final size but left thicker, about three-quarters of the pulling should take place at this stage; it will be completed when on the pot.

7. By using the end, instead of the flat of the thumb, a concave curve or dorsal ridges can be made on one face of the

handle. Considerable practice is needed to do this well.

8. When the pulling has been completed, lay the required length of handle on a clean board and, holding the remaining lump of clay in the left hand, cut the clay off level with the end of the board, using one downward stroke of the right forefinger.

9. Continue making the required number of handles.

10. Leave the handles to firm-up a little, then cross-hatch and coat with slurry the area of the pot to which the handle is to be attached.

11. Hold the top end of the handle in the left hand and by rolling the thumb of the right hand over the cut end, splay it out a little. This gives some extra clay with which to join handle to pot.

12. Support the pot from the inside and holding the handle near the end, press it firmly onto the pot. Weld it to the pot by spreading some of the handle onto the pot. Never make the handle thinner at the joint than elsewhere.

13. Support the pot horizontally in the left hand and continue pulling the handle, removing any irregularities and giving it its final size and cross-section.

14. Supporting the handle, place the pot vertically on the bench. Bow the handle into the required curve and attach the lower end, taking care that the length of handle is correct and that the lower point of attachment is the best possible.

15. Pinch off any surplus length and wipe the end with firm strokes of the thumb.

16. Leave the completed pot to dry. If the handle has a tendency to sag invert the pot; in the case of a jug take care not to damage the lip.

Never fiddle and nurse a handle as this tends to remove the spontaneity and spring that results from the pulling method.

Some potters, instead of using the method described, attach a stub of clay to the pot and do all the pulling from the pot.

It is well worth while attaching numerous handles to one pot as a means of practice, for many excellent pots are spoiled by bad handles.

Lugs

Lugs are handles attached to the side of a pot, such as a casserole and large jars. They are pulled in the same way as a jug handle except that an even, non-tapering strip is pulled with a triangular section. Suitable lengths are cut from the strip and pressed firmly onto a cross-hatched area of the pot. The thumb and fingers of the right hand are wetted and using an oscillating movement the handle is gently squeezed out. The ends are then wiped with firm directed strokes of the thumb.

There are many other types of handle but those described will suffice for most pots in general use.

Turning

Turning is a means of trimming a thrown shape. It is used to remove excess clay from a thickly thrown shape, to make a footring on a bowl and to trim the top of some types of lid before throwing a knob.

Where throwing *makes* a shape, turning involves *working on* a shape that has been made and is rigid. It is better to avoid turning wherever possible as it removes the fluid, plastic lines of the thrown form. Some clays which are short and difficult to throw, such as porcelain, have to be thrown quite thickly and then turned until they are thin. This is one reason why many potters do not choose to use porcelain and one reason for the comparatively high cost of porcelain wares.

While, as a general rule, it is best to avoid turning where possible, some pots can nevertheless greatly benefit from turning. For example, most bowls—large bowls in particular—are greatly improved if they spring up from a turned foot. The foot should be generous, not a mean half-hearted little ring. This means that thought must be given to the foot when throwing, so that sufficient clay is left at the base for such a foot. Cups also benefit from a foot ring as this can fit into the well of a saucer. Plates and saucers are frequently more satisfactory if thrown with a heavy base which can later be turned. This aids the throwing of a flat base, assists in lifting from the wheel and careful turning can reduce the risks of warping during the glaze firing.

Some potters consider that most pots benefit from skimming the base and bottom 25 mm (1 in) or so of the wall. The term 'skimming' is used when very

little clay is to be removed by turning. In simple terms, turning involves using the wheel as a vertical lathe, upon which the leather-hard pot is usually inverted, and a sharp tool is used to cut away the unwanted clay.

When throwing was used as a means of production in the pottery industry, horizontal lathes, similar to a woodworker's and metal worker's lathe, were used. Perhaps this was a relic from the 18th century when goldsmiths founded the first porcelain and bone-china factories.

Basic method of turning

1. Allow the thrown pot to become leather-hard, ensuring that the pot dries evenly by inverting it as soon as it is firm enough. Care must be taken to avoid the rim becoming dry while the base is wet.

2. Prepare a means of holding the pot onto the wheel head which will not damage the pot, in particular the rim.

The method of fixing varies with different types of shapes:

a) bowls, plates, cups, cylindrical pots and lids.

Throw a thin-domed pad of clay onto the wheel. It should be about 2 cm (¾ in) wider than the widest pot to be turned and vary from approximately 1 cm (½ in) thick at the circumference to approximately 5 cm (2 in) in the centre. Smooth the surface and remove all

slurry with a rib. Make a series of concentric circles as guides for centring the pots.

The pot to be turned is placed centrally on the pad and the wheel turned to check any eccentricity. When the pot is central, gently press the pot onto the pad. There is little danger of it coming adrift unless the rim of the pot is dry or the pad gets too firm. In either case dampen the offender. Some flat shapes—such as plates—may need supporting in the centre with a blob of clay to prevent sagging. An alternative to a pad is to centre the bowl on the wheel head then, holding the pot in place, press three blobs of clay against the rim of the pot. This method is useful when only one or two pots have to be turned. Care must be taken to avoid distorting or damaging the rim of the pot.

b) Jugs and large cylinders.

These can be placed on a pad, as just described for bowls etc. Ensure that the pad is soft enough to accommodate the lip of the jug without causing damage.

Care must be taken to support tall pots with the left hand while turning and the wheel must not turn at high speed or else the pot will fly off, giving a demonstration of centrifugal force!

c) Spherical forms and narrow necked pots.

Such shapes cannot be adequately supported on a pad and any attempt to do

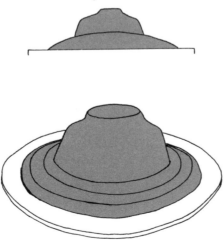

Fig. 23. A turning pad. A shallow dome of clay thrown on the wheel, marked with concentric circles and used for holding pots while they are turned. *Stage 2a and 2b*

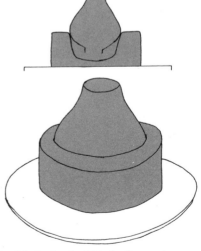

Fig. 24. A chuck. This is thrown to support spherical and narrow necked pots while they are turned. *Stage 2c*

so would probably ruin the pot. They need supporting at the shoulder, in the case of narrow-necked pots, and about one third of the way down from the rim, in the case of a spherical pot. To do this a chuck should be thrown. This is best done when the pots are made so that the chuck can firm-up and if necessary be turned.

Another method of making a chuck is to line a metal cup-head, if this is available, with clay and turn a suitable opening to accept the pot.

3. Select a suitable turning tool or tools for the shape to be turned. Most potters seem to have favourite tools so it is a case of trying them out to find the best. Generally, the expensive stainless steel type are the least satisfactory for they are difficult to keep sharp. Always keep

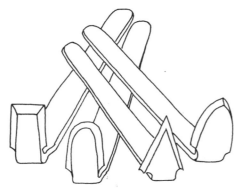

Fig 25. A selection of mild-steel turning tools. These can be bought or made from 5mm ($\frac{3}{16}$ in) steel strip.

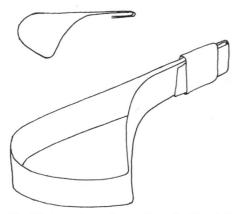

Fig. 26. A turning tool made from the thin steel strip used in packaging. Such tools are easily made by bending the steel with a pair of pliers.

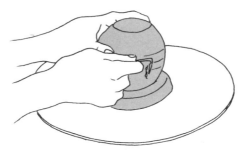

Fig. 27. Turning a spherical pot. The pot is in a shallow chuck and supported by the left hand. The turning tool is held firmly in the right hand.

turning tools sharp; this is best done with a single-cut file.

4. Hold the tool firmly in the right hand, support the pot with the left hand and if possible give the tool additional support with one finger of the left hand. Except when turning tall pots which are only held with a clay pad, rotate the wheel quite quickly and using the point of the tool mark out the area of clay to be pared off.

5. Pare off all the surplus clay. If a foot ring is being cut, do not cut away the inside until the outside shape has been completed; once the inside has been cut away the foot ring cannot be altered. Generally the final outside shape of a pot should follow that of the inside, so giving a wall of even thickness. With experience the required amount of turning can to a large extent be gauged by remembering the inside shape, but any uncertainty can be resolved by lifting the pot from the wheel and checking how much more turning is required. A needle can be used as a gauge for large pots by pushing it into the pot and noting how far it has to be inserted before just emerging inside the pot. Another method of gauging the thickness is to tap the base with the finger and listen to the sound; if thin, the sound will be more resonant.

6. When most of the turning has been completed cut a 45° chamfer at the base, be it a foot ring or a flat base. The size of chamfer depends on the size of the pot, but it will help give the pot a feeling of springing up, prevent chipping and in some cases aid glazing. If a pot is to be only partially glazed, such as leaving a lid gallery unglazed, it is helpful to score a thin line while turning as a guide for glazing.

Chattering

This is a common fault that can occur when turning. The surface of the pot becomes corrugated and the turning tool rides the corrugations instead of removing them. It can be caused by the pot being too hard or soft, by uneven drying of the pot or by the turning tool being held too slackly or at the wrong angle.

The first causes can be avoided by turning the clay when in the right condition. The turning tool must always be held very firmly and the depth of cut obtained is determined by the angle at which it is held to the pot not by exerting pressure. If chattering starts to appear alter the angle of the tool and check that it is not blunt.

It is sometimes difficult for the part-time potter to catch pots in the right condition for turning, but the length of time to leave them in particular conditions can usually be worked out in the light of experience. Quick-drying pots in warm kilns is a risky business as they tend to dry unevenly and are easily forgotten. Some art schools have special drying cabinets which are excellent for they use circulated warm air, not just heat. In the absence of such a luxury it is better to dry pots outside or even by an open window where air can circulate around them.

Plate 22. This striking stoneware piece was made from heavily grogged clay, thrown in sections and assembled.

KILNS

Clay which is sun-dried or even placed in a domestic oven will soften when placed in water. It is only when it is heated to a minimum temperature of approximately 600°C that clay becomes pottery and so is made permanent.

The first firing, which changes clay into pottery, is called a *biscuit-firing* and a second firing, used to melt glazes, is a glaze-firing.

Bonfire Firing

The minimum firing temperature of 600°C can be achieved in a bonfire of dry grass or small pieces of wood. Such a method was used by early man and is still used by many groups of people in Africa, South America and elsewhere. The fuel depends on local availability but it is always dry and light in weight.

The basic procedure is to make the pots, usually by coiling, from a clay that will mature at a low temperature. The pots are invariably of gently curving form, not angular, so that they will most readily withstand thermal shock. The completed pots are thoroughly sun-dried, the larger pots being inverted over a small fire to ensure that they are absolutely dry.

The dry pots are then stacked in a small rounded pile and shards (pieces of broken pots) are placed around the pots to keep the stack steady and to give some protection to the pots. The dry fuel is then placed around and over the stacked pots, and lit. The fire burns through, leaving the pots covered in hot ash. When the pots have cooled, the shards are removed and the fired pots are complete. Some people use sticks to remove the pots while they are still warm so that they can be coated with vegetable matter which leaves a water-proof gum-like coating.

This method of firing can result in about a 30% breakage rate but the Peruvian Indians who fire most of their pots in this way, have few breakages and the clay used is such that it matures at a low temperature, giving a hard resonant pot.

Such firing is ideal for demonstrating to students that firing is essentially, as the name implies, the placing of pots in a fire and not a magic process that takes place in a sophisticated piece of equipment. To avoid breakages it is advisable to use a well-grogged earthen-

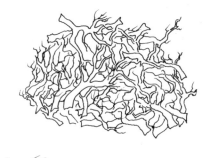

Fig. 28. Bonfire firing. *Bottom:* **the inverted dry pots surrounded with protective shards (broken pots).** *Top:* **the pots have been covered with dry twigs ready for firing.**

ware clay for building the pots and the firing should take place on a dry, wind-free day. If there is a prevailing wind the fire should be shielded with a sheet of iron or other suitable material. As the response of the clay to this brutal treatment is probably unknown, it is advisable to start with a small fire around the pots and gradually build it up until the pots are covered. Small pieces of wood or dry grass should be used, as heavy wood is likely to break the pots. The finished pots will amost certainly be porous and will be pink/red in some areas and black in others, depending on how cleanly the fire burned.

Sawdust Firing

A sawdust firing is a variation of a bonfire firing, and is less dramatic but more suitable for use in primary schools; there is less chance of a pyromaniac setting himself alight! The temperature achieved is usually just sufficient to change the clay into pottery but the ware are invariably fragile and black in colour.

For a school or family that wishes to try pottery but has not got access to a kiln, a sawdust firing is ideal. Any school with a kiln is strongly advised to involve the students in at least one bonfire or sawdust firing as it gives them an understanding of firing that no

KILNS

Fig. 29. Sawdust firing

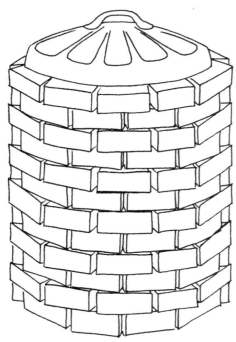

29A: The completed kiln.

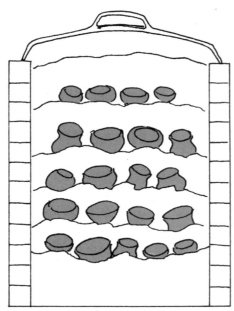

29B: Section through the kiln showing the layers of pots embedded in sawdust.

electric equipment or any amount of lecturing can give.

The procedure is to acquire a couple of sacks of dry sawdust from a local timber merchant or mill, school workshop or butcher's shop. Some butchers use it on the shop floor, and they will usually sell it quite cheaply. The other essential commodity is about 120 bricks; ordinary house bricks are quite satisfactory and second-hand bricks from which the cement has been chipped can usually be found.

A base approximately 1 m (3 ft) square is needed. This can be a slab of concrete, some paving stones or bricks placed on the ground. A brick box, or cylinder approximately 75 cm (2 ft 6 in) square or diameter outside measurement, is then built. Small cracks should be left between the bricks and no cement or other bonding material used.

The kiln is now ready to be loaded with pots. The pots should be small. Pinch pots and small animal figures are ideal. They must be absolutely dry. Sprinkle a layer of sawdust in the kiln about 10 cm (4 in) deep. On this place a layer of pots or figures, allowing space between each pot and between the pots and the kiln bricks. Sprinkle a layer of sawdust over the pots so that the sawdust is about 8 cm (3 in) above the pots. Place another layer of pots on the sawdust. Repeat this procedure of alternate layers of sawdust and pots until the kiln is full. The last layer should be of a generous amount of sawdust.

The kiln is now ready for lighting. This is done at the top, not the bottom, by tucking some newspaper into the top layer of sawdust and lighting it. The sawdust should gently smoulder not flame. If a strong wind is fanning the fire, place a metal dustbin or trash can lid on the top and prop a piece of corrugated iron or similar material against the side of the kiln so that it is screened from the wind.

The kiln should take about a day to fire and should not be disturbed by poking as this will result in broken pots. The work, which will have gently moved to the bottom of the kiln as the sawdust burned away, can then be removed. Some work can be left in its matt black state and the other can be polished with wax polish. Remember, it

is only soft fired and is quite fragile.

Raku Firing

A slightly more sophisticated type of outdoor firing that can be undertaken in schools and by the pottery student is a Raku firing.

Raku bowls are those traditionally used by Japanese Tea-masters. They were introduced into Japan from Korea and were then made in Japan by Korean immigrants from about 1550 A.D. onwards. The early Raku bowls were not made specifically for the Tea ceremony but the esteem in which they were held by the Tea-master encouraged potters to make them specifically for the Tea ceremony.

They are made from a coarse, open clay and are usually made by the pinch pot method or by cutting away a solid block of clay. The clay is invariably too coarse for throwing, although it is possible, and the firing method tends to make slab built and coiled pots come apart. A suitable clay would be a buff or red earthenware clay with large additions of coarse grog or a prepared body like Cranks Mixture. The tea bowls are traditionally asymmetrical due to the method of making but it is best to avoid exaggerating this lack of symmetry. The shapes need to be open and the walls up to 12 mm ($\frac{1}{2}$ in) thick.

The bowls should then be left to dry before biscuit-firing. This firing can be in the Raku kiln or in an electric kiln. If in the Raku kiln, the pots should be packed in fairly tightly, but allowing enough space for the heat to pass through, and the fire should start gently, gradually increasing in intensity until a temperature of between 600 and 900°C is achieved. The nearer it is to 900°C the better. The use of an electric kiln, if one is available, to biscuit-fire, makes things easier and ensures that the pots are fired at 900°C. Purists would no doubt condemn the use of such kilns.

Building a Raku kiln for wood firing

The Raku kiln can be very simply constructed, the method used and shape of the firing chamber varying considerably. The kiln is usually quite small, the firing chamber being about 30 cm (1 ft) square. The essential requisites are that a temperature of about 800°C can be achieved without too great a fuel consumption and that the firing chamber, containing the pots, can be opened, the fired pots removed, others placed in the chamber and the door replaced without great difficulty.

The design of the kiln will depend very much on the type of fuel to be employed. Wood, coal, oil or bottled gas can be used. The traditional Japanese Raku kiln uses charcoal. I have only used wood and oil, so only those fuels are discussed here. Thanks are due to Wally Keeler who developed both the kilns described and the oil burner.

The kiln can be built on a slab of concrete or a brick platform. Approximately 150 bricks are needed. Fire bricks are ideal but these are expensive and if the kiln is only to be used a few times, second-hand house bricks are suitable and probably available free of charge. The floor and roof of the firing chamber are made from kiln shelving which needs to be 60 cm (2 ft) wide and total 90 cm (3 ft) in length. Old kiln shelving should be used; if it is warped and has areas of glaze stuck to it this is no handicap. A thick shelf 20 mm ($\frac{3}{4}$ in) offers better insulation for the roof but this is not essential. The door of the kiln must be readily accessible and this is made easier if a piece of kiln shelf is placed over an opening in the brick wall of the kiln. Having obtained the bricks and some old kiln shelves the kiln can be built as follows:

Make a base 110 cm (3 ft 6 in) long and 80 cm (2 ft 9 in) wide.

Arrange three courses of bricks as shown in the diagram and place a kiln shelf over the opening. Continue building the walls a further three courses but leaving an opening on one side of the kiln, one brick wide and three courses high. Place a kiln shelf over the opening. Note that the space between the end of this second kiln shelf and the wall of the kiln is at the opposite end to that of the first kiln shelf. The opening left between the wall of the kiln and the shelf forming the kiln roof is now reduced in width and a small chimney is built.

If suitable iron bars are available, they can be inserted at the level of the first course of bricks to make fire bars. If such fire bars are not available the kiln can still be fired, although care

Fig. 30. Raku Kiln

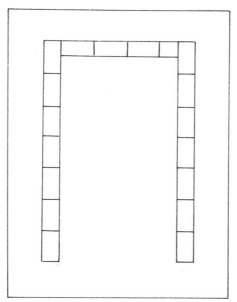

30A: Plan of the kiln showing the base slab (of concrete or bricks) and the arrangement of the first course of bricks.

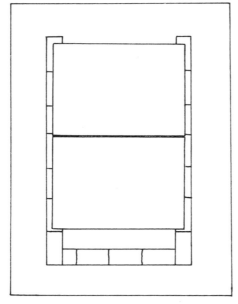

30B: Plan of the kiln after three courses of bricks have been laid and kiln shelving placed over the opening. Note the gap between the kiln shelves and the end wall of the kiln.

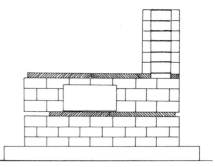

30C: Side view of the completed kiln showing the opening through which the pots will be placed into, and removed from, the firing chamber. The shaded areas indicate the arrangement of kiln shelving.

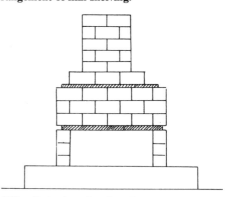

30D: End view showing the arrangement of bricks and kiln shelving.

must be taken not to block up the fire box with ash.

All large cracks and openings in the brickwork and shelving can be filled with a mixture of fire clay and sand, or if no fire clay is available ordinary earthenware or stoneware clay with about 50% of sand added will suffice. The kiln should be thoroughly dry before it is used. The first lot of glazed pots, which must also be dry, can be placed in the kiln and a small fire lit. As the kiln warms and any remaining dampness is driven off the fire can be gradually increased until a roaring flame passes right through the firing chamber. The wood used for fuel must be dry, about 30 cm (1 ft) long and 10 cm (4 in) in diameter.

A pair of long-handled tongs of suitable jaw shape are essential for the task of loading into, and unloading the pots from, the firing chamber.

Special Raku tongs can be bought from potter's merchants, but they can sometimes be borrowed from the metal-work room of a school or college or they can be made from 15 mm ($\frac{1}{2}$ in) steel rod.

When the firing chamber glows red the kiln door can be opened with the tongs and the pots inspected. If the glaze appears smooth and shiny the pots can be removed with the tongs. If the glaze is still matt or is bubbling it has not matured and the pots should be left in the kiln. When the pots are removed from the kiln they can be given a reduced or oxidised finish. If reduction effects are required, the red-hot pots are placed in a metal bucket of sawdust or a similar inflammable material for a few minutes, before plunging the pot into a metal bucket of cold water. If oxidised colours are required the pot can be taken from the kiln and plunged straight into the bucket of water.

The next group of pots, which should have been stood on the kiln to dry thoroughly, can now be picked up with the tongs and placed in the firing chamber and the kiln door replaced. *Never put a damp pot into the kiln* as it is likely to shatter. This procedure is repeated until all the pots are fired. The water will soon become very hot and will need replacing and a constant supply of wood is essential to maintain the temperature in the firing chamber.

A glaze suitable for use with a Raku firing is detailed on page 70. The pots can be glazed all over if this is desired, including the foot as the pots are lifted from the kiln with the tongs while the glaze is still molten. Under and over-glaze painting can both be used effectively, particularly copper oxide, which responds well to the reduction obtained in the sawdust. The reduction makes the body black, and the copper becomes a lustrous copper metal colour.

This type of firing is excellent for demonstrating what happens in a glaze firing, for the glaze can be seen melting, bubbling and finally settling into a smooth, shiny coating. It also shows in a dramatic way the difference between an oxidised and a reduced body and glaze.

However, if used in schools great care and organisation must be used to avoid accidents. It should be stressed that most pots are hot, that the water in which the pots are quenched is hot and that nothing should be picked up before seeking permission. If the firing procedure and the points just mentioned are explained to the students there is no reason why such a firing should not be quite safe.

Raku kilns for oil firing

An alternative fuel to wood is oil. This is less interesting to use but quicker than wood. To buy a burner and air-compressor is expensive but a simple burner can be made with a minimum of equipment and a vacuum cleaner can be used in place of a compressor.

I have used such a kiln in a secondary (high) school on a number of occasions without any mishaps.

The burner is made from a 60 cm (2 ft) length of 32 mm ($1\frac{1}{4}$ in) diameter copper piping, a 90° elbow, an 80 cm (2 ft 8 in) length of 6 mm ($\frac{1}{4}$ in) diameter thin copper piping and a 32 mm ($1\frac{1}{4}$ in) diameter cap over the end of the piping. The narrow pipe is pinched at the end so that it will give a flat fan-like jet of oil and an opening of similar shape is cut in the cap but about 1.5 mm ($\frac{1}{16}$ in) larger all round. A 6 mm ($\frac{1}{4}$ in) hole is drilled in the 90° elbow. The burner is assembled as shown in the diagram and all the joints are soldered. A piece of the 6 mm ($\frac{1}{4}$ in) tubing is also inserted and soldered into a gallon (4.5 litres) paraffin can.

The only other equipment required is a vacuum cleaner, the tube of which is

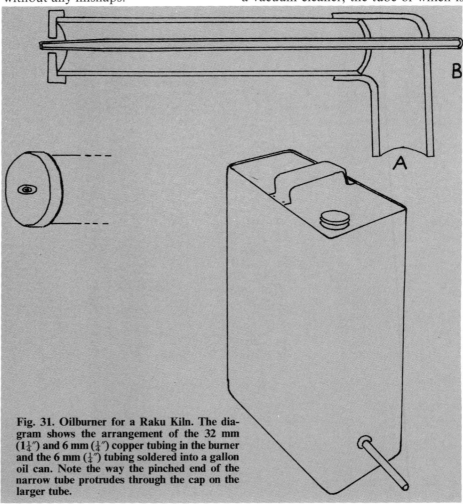

Fig. 31. Oilburner for a Raku Kiln. The diagram shows the arrangement of the 32 mm ($1\frac{1}{4}''$) and 6 mm ($\frac{1}{4}''$) copper tubing in the burner and the 6 mm ($\frac{1}{4}''$) tubing soldered into a gallon oil can. Note the way the pinched end of the narrow tube protrudes through the cap on the larger tube.

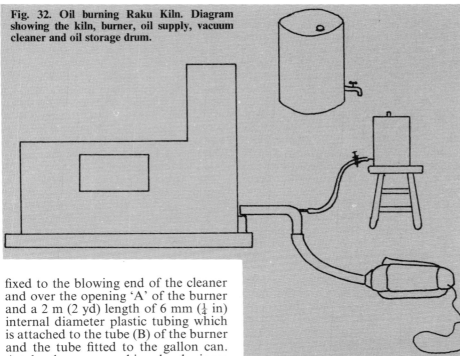

Fig. 32. Oil burning Raku Kiln. Diagram showing the kiln, burner, oil supply, vacuum cleaner and oil storage drum.

fixed to the blowing end of the cleaner and over the opening 'A' of the burner and a 2 m (2 yd) length of 6 mm ($\frac{1}{4}$ in) internal diameter plastic tubing which is attached to the tube (B) of the burner and the tube fitted to the gallon can. A tube clamp, as used in school science laboratories is also required to squeeze the plastic tube and so control the flow of fuel.

The burner is then arranged as shown, taking care to keep the oil as far away as possible from the kiln fire-mouth and to keep the gallon oil can about 60 cm (2 ft) above the burner so as to get a satisfactory gravity feed. Up to eight gallons (36 litres) of domestic fuel oil will be required to fire such a Raku kiln. This is best kept away from the kiln except when topping up the gallon can. Paraffin can be used instead of domestic fuel oil. Never use petrol (gasoline).

To light the kiln, place some paper and dry sticks in the kiln fire-mouth and light them. Place the end of the burner at, but not in, the fire-mouth. When the sticks are well alight turn on the vacuum cleaner and slowly release the tube clamp until a small flame is blown into the fire box. As the kiln warms up, the flow of oil, and so the flame, can be increased. If too much oil is allowed to flow the result will be black smoke! It is only when the kiln starts to glow red inside that the flame can be lengthened to pass through the firing chamber to the base of the chimney.

When the kiln door is opened to remove or place pots in the firing chamber the oil flow should be reduced, increasing the flow when the door has been replaced. It is advisable to wear asbestos gauntlets, if available, as such a kiln may reach 1,000°C.

As with a wood-fired Raku kiln, those participating should be fully aware of the heat involved and only appointed students should be allowed near the burner and oil can. Care should also be taken to ensure that the oil-can, burner and vacuum cleaner cannot be kicked or moved; a no-man's-land around these items is probably necessary. If such safety precautions are taken such a firing is ideal for schools. A dry day is obviously needed both to aid enjoyment and to ensure that the electricity supply to the vacuum cleaner is safe.

Earthenware and Stoneware kilns

While the outdoor kilns described are excellent for obtaining particular effects and explaining what firing is about, they are not normally suitable for firing large quantities of pots nor are they suitable for obtaining the higher temperatures required for earthenware and stoneware firings. This does not mean that suitable outdoor kilns cannot be built.

The two fuels most frequently used in schools and colleges and by the serious amateur are electricity and gas. Many professional potters use oil or wood but such kilns are usually large and need not concern us in this book.

Oxidation and Reduction

Oxidising and reducing atmospheres are referred to in the text and in the list of glaze recipes so these terms need to be explained.

To burn hydro-carbon fuels such as coal, oil, wood and gas, two additional things are needed—heat to start the fire (usually provided by a match), and an adequate supply of oxygen. This oxygen is provided from the air which is either blown into or drawn into the kiln. It is by controlling the supply of air to the kiln that the atmosphere in the firing chamber can be varied. If there is an ample supply of air the flames in the kiln will be clean and smoke-free and the temperature in the kiln should rise steadily. If the supply of air and consequently oxygen is gradually reduced the flames will become lazy, slightly smoky and the unburned gases will start to smell. These gases will light when they come into contact with air, so causing flames to come from the chimney, the spy hole and any other gaps.

While in the firing chamber these oxygen-hungry gases search for oxygen, and the less stable oxides in the clay body and in the glazes give up some of their oxygen. The unstable oxides which show the greatest colour change are iron and copper.

Iron is usually in the form of red iron, i.e. Ferric oxide (Fe_2O_3). This is reduced to Ferrous oxide (FeO), which is grey/green in colour. If iron is present in a glaze in small quantities, up to 2%, all the Ferric oxide becomes Ferrous oxide and so the grey/green celadon glazes are obtained. If large quantities of iron are present not all is reduced so the colour change is not so dramatic.

Copper is usually in the form of Cupric oxide (CuO), which produces green in oxidation. This is reduced to

KILNS

Cuprous oxide (Cu_2O) which gives pink and reds.

In addition to altering the colour of glazes, a reduction firing also affects the surfaces of some glazes, making them smoother and satiny. This change has not yet been explained in scientific terms. The clay body, which invariably contains iron, is also changed in colour by reduction from a buff/brown to a grey/black, although this is only apparent if a fired pot is broken, the surface having reoxidised on cooling to a brown colour.

To summarise:

An oxidised firing is one where there is an ample supply of air for the fuel to burn efficiently and cleanly or where large amounts of air are not required, such as in an electric kiln.

A reduction firing is one where the supply of air is reduced, so causing some metal oxides to be reduced in their oxygen content. All kilns using inflammable fuels can be adjusted to produce such a firing.

Electric kilns

Electric kilns are clean, reliable and easy to operate. They are cheaper to buy and install than gas kilns but cost about the same to operate. They do not require any sort of flue so they can be installed in any room that is well ventilated, has a floor strong enough to support the weight of the kiln and is not a fire hazard. If a kiln is to be installed in a school it is desirable to have it in a separate room, such as a large store-room or if it has to be in the working room it should be fenced off with a rail and this area should be inaccessible unless the students fully understand when the kiln may and may not be opened.

There are only two main types of kiln: front loading and top loading. A front loader has a hinged door on the front like a cupboard, and is packed with pots from the front. A top loader, has a lid which is hinged and is opened to give access from the top. The top loader requires less iron framing and is consequently cheaper than the front loader. Some people consider the top loader more difficult to pack with pots, but after two or three packings it is no more difficult than a front loader. It does however require more bending

down on the part of the packer.

If a sufficient amount of money is available, a front loader is probably to be preferred but as there is frequently a shortage of funds, a top loader is frequently a better buy. Always get a kiln that is likely to be big enough for the size and number of pots that are likely to be made in the next few years. Kilns have a long life. Ensure that the kiln, in particular its elements, are suitable for the type of firings that are anticipated. Stoneware is recommended throughout this book, although earthenware should not be excluded, so a kiln that will fire up to 1,300°C is recommended. This means that elements made from Kanthal A1 wire will be used.

The major disadvantage of electric kilns is the fact that they are only suitable for oxidised firings. Some writers claim that electric kilns can be used for reduction firing and there are methods of achieving such an atmosphere in the kiln, but it is seldom reliable or satisfactory. In addition, the life of the elements is greatly reduced, the nickel oxide which forms on the elements being partly removed in a reducing atmosphere and this can cause arcing and the loss of the element.

It is more difficult to obtain good stoneware glazes in an oxidising kiln, but it certainly is not impossible; very pleasing and reliable glazes have and can be developed for such firings. They are excellent for earthenware glazes. For the busy pottery teacher, without a Technical Assistant, electric kilns are easier to cope with than a gas kiln and a non-specialist can be asked to turn the kiln on or off.

Gas Kilns

Gas kilns are in many ways to be preferred for they can be regulated to give oxidising and reducing atmospheres. The latter permits lustre glazes to be used in the earthenware range, and stoneware glazes requiring a reducing atmosphere, such as the celadons. Gas kilns are reliable and once understood, easy to regulate. They, like electric kilns, can be depended upon to reach a temperature in more or less a given time. They are suitable for temperatures up to 1,300°C and unlike electric kilns have no elements that wear out and require replacement.

The main disadvantages of gas kilns are the comparatively high initial cost and finding suitable accommodation. The initial cost is higher than that of an electric kiln due to the necessary provision of a large gas supply pipe, the installation of a flue pipe and the kiln structure is much heavier. A gas kiln must be installed in an adequately ventilated room which permits a chimney to rise above the kiln. Such a chimney is usually made of metal as a considerable amount of heat, as well as fumes, pass through it. Due to the fumes generated during a reduction firing, a gas kiln should not be installed in a workroom but should either be in a room specifically for kilns or in a well-ventilated store-room.

Most gas kilns are front loading and invariably of the down-draught type although top loading kilns do exist. Down-draught means that the flames and heat are not permitted to just pass through the firing chamber and out through a chimney situated at the top but are made to rise to the roof of the firing chamber, back down through the pots, passing through spaces in the kiln floor and finally out through flues connected to the chimney. Such kilns are far more efficient and permit much higher temperatures to be achieved that the up-draught type.

The main choice, apart from size, available in gas kiln operation is between one which relies on natural draught and one that has an air supply blown by an electric fan. The blown air type is based on industrial models and has the advantage of offering accurate control of air and gas by adjusting taps. Another advantage is the fact that it is almost unaffected by winds and draughts. Its great disadvantages are the continual noise of the fan and the high initial cost.

The natural draught type is more common and relies on being built in a position which is free of down-draughts from roofs, and adjustment is by dampers for secondary air and venturi for primary air fitted to the burners. Such kilns can be affected by strong winds but once understood, they are quite simple to fire.

All gas kilns, like wood and oil-fired kilns require understanding and practice before the required rate of temperature rise and degree of reduction is achieved. A few early disappointments must be accepted as part of the learning process. All manufacturers provide firing instructions.

Primary air is that which enters the kiln with the gas or any other carbon fuel and so permits that fuel to burn. Secondary air enters the kiln at a point where the fuel is already burning and permits secondary combustion of the partly burned gases.

ANCILLARY AND SAFETY EQUIPMENT

Electric Kilns

Most electric kilns are supplied with a control switch giving low, medium and high ratings so no ancillary equipment is essential although some can be helpful. If the kiln is to be used in a school some sort of safety device should be fitted so that the students cannot be electrocuted if the kiln door is opened. The simplest and cheapest is to fit a padlock to the door. Another way is to fit a door switch which turns off the power supply when the door is opened; it does not prevent burning if the kiln is hot. If a door switch and padlock are fitted the students should be quite safe. There are other more sophisticated and expensive safety devices available, but those mentioned, plus awareness on the part of the students of the dangers of burning and electrocution, should be quite sufficient.

Students should be encouraged to help with kiln stacking and unstacking, for this is as much a part of pottery as making the pots, but it should only be undertaken after careful tuition and supervision.

The low/medium/high switch can be replaced by an energy regulator which gives greater control of the rate of rise in temperature and permits a more even firing. A thermocouple and pyrometer are very useful in judging the rate of rise in temperature and for indicating when the kiln has reached the desired temperature. A pyrometer should always be tested by comparing the temperature indicated with pyrometric cones, and cones should always be used when glaze firing.

Although pyrometers are frequently inaccurate they are invariably consistent, so that once the inaccuracy has been noted the pyrometer can be very useful. It is possible to fit a programme controller to electric and gas kilns which will control the rate of rise in temperature and turn the kiln off when a pre-set temperature has been reached. Such equipment can be useful in a school situation where the teacher has little time to keep checking kilns but such equipment is very costly and if a list of priorities had to be drawn up, equipment such as a controller, would not be at the top of the list.

Gas Kilns

Gas kilns are supplied with the essential control taps. As with electric kilns a wide range of ancillary equipment is available. A water gauge, which indicates the pressure of the gas entering the burners is useful if the control taps are to be accurately used for consistent firings. For the individual potter no other extra kiln equipment is necessary, but a school kiln needs to be fitted with a door lock and if the kiln is likely to be left on overnight to pre-heat, as is often necessary in order to reach the required temperature during the following day, a safety device which will turn off the gas in the event of the flame blowing out must be fitted. Failure to do this could result in an unfortunate explosion.

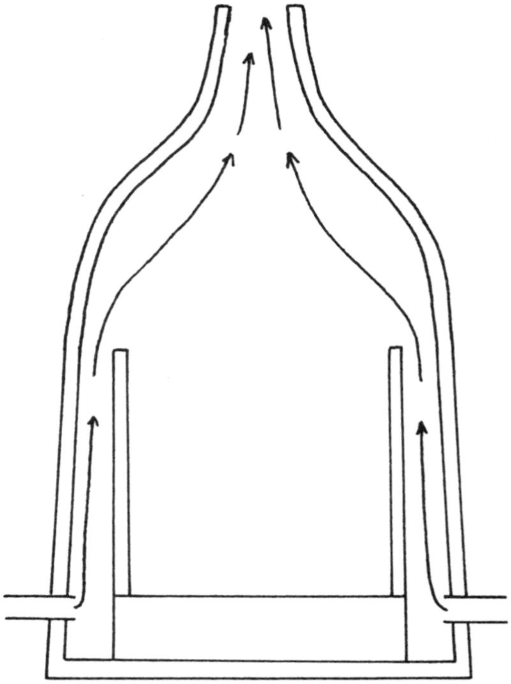

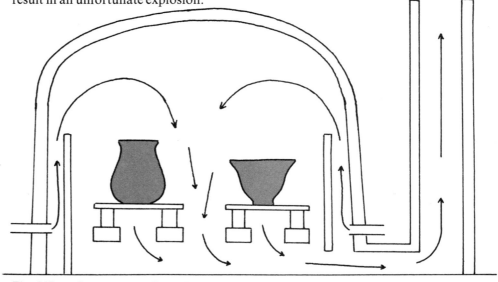

Fig. 33A. An Up-draught Kiln. The arrows indicate the direction of the flames. They pass outside bag-walls and straight up through the chimney. Not all up-draught kilns have bag walls.

Fig. 33B. A Down-draught Kiln. The arrows indicate the direction of the flames. They pass outside bag walls and are then drawn down between the pots, under the kiln chamber floor and then up through the chimney.

STACKING AND FIRING THE KILN

Most pots are fired twice. The first firing, the biscuit-firing, changes the clay into pottery. The second firing, the glaze firing, melts the glaze which is applied to the biscuit-fired pot and either wholly or partly vitrifies the clay. Some pots made by studio potters and by industrial manufacturers have glaze applied before being fired and are then once-fired. Due to the difficulties posed by this method in a school situation it is not discussed here.

Biscuit-firing

When pots or sculptural forms have been made they must be left to become thoroughly dry before they are fired. Large pots may take more than two weeks, depending on the thickness of the pot and drying conditions. If a pot is only slightly damp when fired, it will probably crack or shatter, so ruining the pot and endangering the pots around it.

Assuming that there is adequate kiln shelving and props upon which to stand them, kiln stacking can be a fascinating challenge to use every available space without endangering the pots.

1. Sort out the pots into groups of about the same height. This can be done by actually moving the pots into groups or by remembering how many pots of a given size await firing.

It is usually more convenient to stack small pots near the top and medium-sized pots at the bottom of the kiln, so preventing an over-heated area. Really tall pieces should go to the top of the kiln, where the taller stilts will be more secure.
2. Place three kiln props about 1 cm ($\frac{1}{2}$ in) taller than the pots to be stacked, so that they form a triangle as shown in the illustration. Three props give the shelf

better support and are more stable than four props. This will prolong the life of the shelves.
3. Stack the pots onto the shelf. In a biscuit-firing the pots may touch each other but not the kiln wall. Small pots may be placed inside larger pots but they must stand evenly and there must be no danger of one pot getting jammed inside another after the contraction that will occur in the firing. Pots can also be stacked rim to rim, foot to foot if they are of the same diameter. This is useful when stacking repetition-thrown bowls or mugs.

Flat pots such as plates should always be stacked with extra care, never having other pots placed on them. It is advisable to raise the foot up on small wads of clay and alumina (50:50), ensuring that there are sufficient wads to prevent the pot warping. This will allow the heat to pass under as well as over the pot and so prevent an uneven temperature rise and consequent breakage.
4. When one shelf has been filled the next shelf is placed on the props and the group of three props is then placed immediately above the preceding props. It is essential that the props form continuous columns separated by the shelves. Failure to do this can cause shelves to break or warp during firing.

If some of the pots are of porcelain or another white clay, take care that the

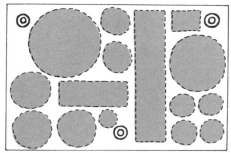

Fig. 34A. Plan of a kiln shelf, showing the arrangement of pots and kiln props.

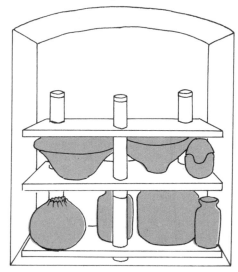

Fig. 34B. Front view of partially stacked kiln, showing position of the three kiln props.

Plate 23. A kiln stacked both expertly and economically. Note staggered shelves.

pots are not made dirty by rubbing them against a pot made of a non-white clay.

5. When stacking a kiln that has more than one bank of shelves it is essential to stagger the height of the front shelves from those at the back. If the front and back shelves are stacked in line with one another the effect is to cut the kiln into horizontal layers, so causing uneven firing temperatures.

6. When stacking the front of the kiln ensure that space is left for the temperature cones to stand where they can be seen through the spyhole in the kiln door.

7. Kiln shelves are kept flatter and their useful life prolonged if they are turned over each time they are used. This is made easier if the corner of each new shelf is marked with a small cross. A mixture of iron oxide and water is suitable for making the mark. Once a shelf is really warped it is inadvisable to reverse it in an attempt to flatten it as this can cause it to break during the firing.

Biscuit-firing temperatures

The temperature to which a biscuit-firing is taken, and the rate of rise in temperature vary considerably. As the last major chemical change and shock to the clay occurs at about 980°C this is generally the most suitable maximum temperature for biscuit-firing. If the clay body is still very soft and too porous at 980°C the firing temperature should be increased until the ware is stronger but still suitably porous to absorb the glaze. Some potters biscuit-fire in about five hours but this is risky unless experience has proved that such a rapid firing is suitable for the clay body being used; this will only be apparent after glaze firing. A firing cycle lasting 10 hours is more usual and safer. Many potters prefer to leave the kiln on 'low' or at energy regulator setting '10', overnight, then turn the kiln to 'medium' or reg. 50 for about two hours before putting the kiln full on until 980°C is reached.

The spy-hole and top ventilator, if there is one, should be left open until 600°C is reached so that all gases from carbonaceous matter and the chemically combined water can escape. For the same reasons, top-loading kilns should be propped open about 2 cm (1 in) with a piece of thin kiln shelf. Care must be taken to ensure that the kiln is still safe. If the kiln is not in a separate lockable room, a chain or bracket should be available to lock the kiln lid into position and prevent the kiln being opened by unauthorised persons.

If the kiln is in a school and it is necessary to complete a firing during school hours, the only way is to leave the kiln on low overnight, turn to medium on arrival at school, say 8.30, and turn to full-on at about 10.30. The firing will then be completed during the afternoon, the time depending on the type and size of kiln.

The kiln should not be opened until the temperature has fallen to about 200°C.

Glaze-firing

The procedure for stacking a glaze-firing is similar to that for a biscuit-firing. The major difference is that all the pots must be placed separately without any part of one pot touching another. This means that fewer pots can be stacked into a glaze-firing than can be stacked into a biscuit-firing.

Stoneware

When stacking work for a stoneware firing, check that the glaze has been properly wiped off the foot or base of each piece, and that the glaze has not been applied too thickly, so risking a run of glaze onto the kiln shelf. It is advisable to dust each shelf with a thin coating of placing sand, taking care not to get any on or in the pots. This will prevent the clay sticking to the shelves and lessen the risk of any glaze doing the same. Dusting the shelf with sand is preferable to a batt wash, as the latter does not allow the kiln shelf to be reversed for each firing. However, if a pot is not properly cleaned at the base or if the glaze is much too thickly applied nothing will prevent the pot and shelf being ruined. Good glaze application is essential.

As with the biscuit-firing, ensure that the temperature cones will be seen through the spy-hole.

Earthenware

Earthenware that is to be used as functional table-ware is best glazed all over, including the base. Therefore, each pot must be stood on a stilt. Stilts are available in many sizes and one or more of a suitable size to give the pot support on the foot ring or where the wall of the pot joins the base, should be used. The stilts are soon knocked from the pot after firing and the razor-sharp remains can be removed with a small carborundum stone. Except for the use of stilts, earthenware stacking is the same as that for stoneware.

Glaze-firing temperatures

Glaze-firing temperatures vary enormously—from low earthenware at 1,000°C to high stoneware at 1,300°C. The temperature will be dictated by the glazes used, so the following, based on experience, is advice applicable to most glaze-firings.

Ensure that the glazes used for a particular firing all mature at about the same temperature. It is obviously impossible to fire a glaze maturing at 1,280°C and a glaze maturing at 1,000°C in the same kiln. To avoid confusion it is better only to use glazes that mature at one temperature or, at the most, one earthenware temperature and one stoneware temperature.

If an electric kiln is to be used for stoneware firings it is better to use glazes maturing at 1,260°–1,280°C rather than 1,300°C, as this will prolong the life of the kiln elements.

The firing cycle for a glaze kiln can be quicker than that for a biscuit-firing as there is no carbonaceous matter to burn out of the clay. However, many authorities consider it advisable not to allow the temperature to climb by much more than 100°C per hour, particularly between 500°C and 600°C, when the quartz inversion occurs. While it is both safer for the pots and better for some glazes if the average rise in temperature is about 100°C per hour it is possible to have satisfactory firings with the initial rise in temperature averaging 300°C per hour, with the rate of rise slowing down as the firing proceeds.

The rate of rise in temperature is primarily dictated by the size and type of kiln. A large kiln, .425m³ (15 cu ft) plus, will take 24 hours or more to fire, while some small kilns will reach 1,280°C in about six hours. Most kiln manufacturers supply charts and instructions suggesting the rate of climb obtainable and the necessary gas or electricity settings required.

Gas kilns and reduction

Gas kiln manufacturers usually provide instructions for controlling the kiln atmosphere of their particular design of kiln. Reduction should not commence until the kiln has reached 1,000°C and the initial reduction should not be too heavy as this will result in dull glazes, a drop in kiln temperature and in extreme cases of over-reduction, to clouds of smoke and a possible explosion when air is re-introduced into the firing chamber.

If over-reduction does cause clouds of smoke or the burners to go out, turn off the gas and restrict the air supply until all the smoke has cleared. Then, gradually allow air to enter the firing chamber, so completely clearing smoke and fumes from the kiln. The burners can then be re-lit and the firing continued.

> NEVER re-light a gas kiln if it goes out without ensuring that all the unburned gas in the kiln has been dispersed.
> NEVER suddenly increase the air supply to a very smoky reducing kiln.

Only experiment and careful recording will enable a particular kiln to give the required results at the minimum cost for, while the final temperature and the rate of rise can be measured by a pyrometer and temperature cones and recorded, the amount of reduction has to be judged by eye. A lazy flame, which meanders among the pots, is desirable, and for kilns using natural gas I have found that fairly heavy reduction is necessary if some pots are not to be partially reduced. The flame that comes from the spy-hole will be blue for a light reduction and cream for a very heavy, smoky reduction. Midway between a light and heavy reduction the flame will be blue with an orange/red tip. I find such a middle course gives the best results.

If the temperature starts to fall when the kiln is first adjusted for a reducing atmosphere, more air should be admitted, thus giving a lighter reduction. The rate of rise in temperature will be less for a reduction firing but the temperature must not be allowed to fall.

When the kiln has almost reached the required temperature it is frequently beneficial to have a brief oxidising fire, lasting 15–30 minutes. This will improve the colour of the clay body as it causes the iron to re-oxidise on the surface, so making the clay warmer and richer in colour. Beware! The temperature rise can be rapid when re-oxidising at the end of a reduction firing, so care must be taken not to over-fire.

Cooling

When the firing has reached the required temperature the gas or electricity is turned off and the pots left to cool. Many stoneware glazes are improved if the cooling, down to 800°C, is rapid. Iron-rich glazes, such as Tenmuku, tend to have a more varied colour, ranging from red to black, if cooled rapidly, as opposed to a crystalline red/brown when cooled slowly. Glazes containing titanium dioxide are also improved as the titanium has less chance of recrystallising and so becoming matt.

Rapid cooling also allows the impatient potter to see his finished work a little earlier!

When the temperature reaches 800°C the kiln dampers must be closed and the rate of cooling slowed, for rapid cooling between 800°C and 300°C can cause dunting—that is, the pot can be split. When the temperature is down to about 300°C the kiln door and dampers can be opened, and the pots removed when they are cool enough to handle.

Temperature Cones

Temperature-indicating cones are essential for checking the temperature in the kiln. They are sometimes called Seger cones—after the German chemist who developed them—or Staffordshire cones and sometimes after the name of their manufacturer. Cones are made of glaze material carefully formulated to bend after being subjected to a given amount of heat work; that is, they respond in the same way as glazes. A given temperature held for a longer time has the same effect on glazes as a slightly higher temperature held for a shorter time. It is the fact that cones give a better indication of glaze behaviour that makes them so much better than a pyrometer for glaze firing.

A wide range of cones is manufactured, easily covering the firing range likely to be needed in the pottery, and

Table of the principal changes occurring during the firing and cooling of a kiln.

FIRING

110°	Atmospheric water given off. Pots are now dry.
220	Cristobolite inversion.
300	Most organic matter burned out.
450	Chemically combined H_2O given off up to 600°.
573	Free quartz changes from alpha to beta form.
600	Clay just becoming ceramic.
800	Sintering begins.
980	Sharp shrinkage. Formation of mullite begins, giving the body strength.
	Biscuit-firing completed for most clays.
1,000	Melt in the clay pulls particles together, causing shrinkage. Soft earthenware glazes melted.
	Stoneware reduction can begin.
1,100	Hard earthenware glazes melted.
1,200	Cristobolite begins to be formed.
	Vitrification of red clay.
1,300	Most stoneware clays vitrified.
	Stoneware glazes melted.
	Stoneware firings completed between 1,250°–1,300°C.

COOLING

1,200°	Glazes become increasingly viscous (non-liquid).
	Crystallisation in glazes down to 0°C.
	Rapid cooling of kiln can take place to help quality of glazes and colour of clay body.
1,000	Clay body becomes solid.
800	Rapid cooling not safe below this temperature.
600	Dunting (cracking) danger to clay, particularly if cooled unevenly.
600	Glaze begins to craze if it does not fit the clay body.
573	Quartz inversion from beta to alpha.
220	Cristobolite inversion.
	Kiln can be unpacked.

they are made in two sizes—standard and miniature. For the majority of kilns the standard size is the most useful, but for small kilns and kilns with a very small spy-hole the miniature size is very useful. It is normal to place three cones—one bending at the required temperature for the firing and two bending at successively lower temperatures. The two cones bending below the required temperature give warning that the firing is nearing completion and that frequent checks are required.

It is obviously essential to ensure that the cones will be visible through the spy-hole. It is amazing how many potters and teachers fail to take this necessary precaution. If a kiln is new or the potter is new to the kiln, it is advisable to place additional cones at the top, centre and bottom of the firing chamber and check the cones as the kiln is unstacked, to discover if the kiln fires evenly. If it is uneven, those glazes preferring a higher or lower firing can be placed accordingly.

Some experienced potters judge whether a biscuit-firing is complete by the colour, but few choose not to use cones for glaze-firings.

GLAZING

CHAPTER 9

Why do we glaze?

Pots are glazed to enhance their form and offer a variation in colour and texture that clay alone cannot give. For functional wares glaze offers a smooth and hygienic surface. Low-fired wares such as earthenware, which are porous, are made more impervious and so suitable for table-ware.

Stoneware is, therefore, glazed for aesthetic reasons and to make it more hygienic in use. It is usually impervious without being glazed. The surface of stoneware glazes ranges from hard, shiny and functional to dry, matt and decorative. The colour range is subdued but extensive and includes the brown/black Tenmuku glazes, the delicate blue Ying-Ching celadons and the soft white of dolomite glazes. For table-ware crazing should be avoided but it can enhance and decorate porcelain. It is often desirable to leave some areas unglazed, so giving a contrast between the clay and the glaze.

Earthenware is glazed above all to make it hygienic and impervious so that it can be used for table-ware. It should be glazed all over, none of the clay being left unglazed. Earthenware glazes tend to be shiny and not very interesting in texture but they can show brushed decoration and slip decoration to great advantage and a wide range of colours, often bright, can be achieved. A non-crazing glaze is essential.

Glazing should never be an afterthought or a process to be carried out in a hurry. In many respects glazing is more difficult than making the pot. While making the pot, it is possible to make adjustments to the form. The process is not irreversible, the unfired pot can always be rejected and returned to the clay bin.

Glazes, in their unfired state, give no indication of their final colour or texture, and once committed to the glaze firing, no adjustments can be made. The pot might well last a thousand years! Only experience will enable glazes to be understood and the most suitable glaze chosen for a particular pot. A notebook recording the glazes used, and the results, is essential if glazes are to be understood and used to enhance the beauty and form of the pots being produced.

What is a glaze?

In simplified terms, a glaze is a glassy coating applied to a pot. A more technical definition would be: Glaze is one of a group of vitreous substances called *glasses*, which are supercooled liquids of high viscosity at ordinary temperatures. Such *glasses* can be formed by a number of inorganic oxides, silica being the most important.

Such a definition is rather technical for those without a scientific education, so an attempt must be made to explain it. Glass is, in one major aspect the exception to a scientific rule. Most materials can exist as a gas, a liquid or a solid depending on temperature. Water is a typical example, for below $0°C$ it is a solid (ice), between $0°C$ and $100°C$ it is a liquid, above $100°C$ it starts to become a gas (steam). When in the solid state most materials have a crystalline structure, but glass does not have a crystalline structure; it retains some of the characteristics of a liquid. It may be considered as a liquid that has cooled and solidified without re-crystallising.

Glass will eventually crystallise but this may take many hundreds of years. Such crystallisation can be observed as an iridescence on the surface of Roman glass and the lead-glazed wares of the Chinese Han dynasty.

The most important of the glass-forming oxides is silica which is the basis of all glasses. It would make an excellent hard and durable glaze by itself but for the fact that it has a melting point of $1,710°C$. It is sometimes used but the difficulty of melting it at such a high temperature makes it impractical and too expensive for general use. This means that the melting point of the silica has to be reduced by adding fluxes. The most commonly used fluxes are soda and lime. When given proportions of silica, soda and lime are heated they will liquefy at or below $1,500°C$. If the melt is too fluid for the glass worker to fashion his wares, small amounts of alumina are added to make the glass more viscous, i.e. sticky and less inclined to run.

It is sometimes asked: 'Why cannot glass be ground and applied to a pot as a glaze?' This would almost certainly be unsatisfactory for two reasons. It would be too fluid and would run down the pot onto the kiln shelf, and it would craze, that is, on cooling the glass would contract more than the clay and would be full of small cracks. Crazing does not occur in glass-making as the glass is free to contract without the resistance of another material such as clay.

The difference between glass and glaze
Glass is thus too fluid during the melt to be useful as a glaze, but additions of alumina reduce the fluidity and increase the viscosity (stickiness) of the glass. Suitable additions of alumina will enable the glass to melt but stay on the pot; so a glaze is basically a glass with a comparatively high amount of alumina. The ratio of alumina to silica is usually between 1:5 and 1:10.

Another distinction between glass and a glaze is that glass is melted in a vat whereas glaze has to be mixed from the raw materials and applied to the surface of the pottery before being melted in the kiln.

A problem presented by glazes but not glass is that of crazing. Sometimes in stoneware pottery the fine cracks of crazing are accepted as decoration, but with earthenware and functional stoneware crazing is best eliminated. This involves taking great care when selecting suitable fluxes for lowering the melting point of the glaze.

To sum up: a glaze is a high alumina glass coating melted onto a clay form.

What must a glaze contain?
There are three necessary elements in a glaze:

1. Silica (SiO_2)
This is the principal glass-forming material. Silica alone would form a glaze but for the fact that its melting point is 1,700°C and most clays can only be fired between 1,000°C and 1,300°C. To lower this high melting point a FLUX must be added.

2. Flux
A flux is a compound which has the effect of lowering the melting point of the glaze. More than one flux can be used in a glaze. In fact a better glaze melt is obtained if more than one flux *is* used.

Examples of flux used in stoneware glazes:

Potassium Oxide K_2O
Sodium Oxide Na_2O
Calcium Oxide CaO

Examples of flux used in earthenware glazes:

Lead Oxide *PbO*
Potash K_2O
Sodium Na_2O
Calcium *CaO*

3. A refractory element
A glaze made from just silica and a flux is soft and runny, and only suitable for low temperature glazes, which to obtain specific colouring effects must be free of alumina.

The refractory element is added to form a stronger glaze that is more viscous when being fired.

Examples of such materials:
Aluminiun Oxide Al_2O_3
Titanium Oxide TiO_2

It would not be practical for potters to use refined and pure materials, the compounds used, therefore, are those commonly found in nature and they usually provide more than one element.

The four most common stoneware glaze ingredients are:

China Clay (Al_2O_3 $2SiO_2$ $2H_2O$)
This is made up of:

Alumina 1 part. *A refractory material.*
Silica 2 parts. *A glass former.*
Water 2 parts. *This will burn out as a gas.*

Potash Felspar (K_2O Al_2O_3 $6SiO_2$)
Potash 1 part. *A flux*
Alumina 1 part. *A refractory material.*
Silica 6 parts. *A glass former.*

Whiting ($CaCO_3$) *Also known as lime.*
This provides:
Calcium *A flux*

Wood Ash
The chemical analysis of wood ash varies greatly with the type of wood and the area in which it is grown, but such ashes contain:

Alumina 2–15% *A refractory material*
Silica 30–80% *A glass former*
Potash 1–15% *A flux*
Soda 2–10% *A flux*
Lime 2–30% *A flux*

plus iron oxide, phosphorous, magnesium and other elements. This indicates that ash can provide all the requirements of a glaze.

Together these materials provide a glass former (silica), fluxes (potash, lime, soda) and a refractory material

(alumina). They can therefore be used together but not necessarily all together, to form a glaze. It is the proportions in which these materials are used that determine the melting point and the quality of the resultant glaze. The proportion of materials giving the lowest melting point is known as the *eutectic*.

Many other materials can be used to obtain various surface textures and colour responses. For example magnesium—which can be provided in the form of magnesium carbonate or as talc—gives the glaze a buttery surface and tends to make cobalt oxide turn purple instead of blue.

Line Blends
The best way of understanding the way in which different materials behave and affect each other is to carry out a number of simple tests known as line blends. Such tests compare either the reaction of two materials when mixed in different proportions or the reaction of a constant mixture of materials when another material is added in different proportions.

To carry out such tests a strip of clay about 20 cm (8 in) × 5 cm (2 in) × 1 cm ($\frac{3}{8}$ in) is cut out and eleven indentations about 6 mm ($\frac{1}{4}$ in) are made with the finger. It is not essential to have eleven indentations but it simplifies the calculations.

									Strip No. 1	
1	2	3	4	5	6	7	8	9	10	11

Each impression should be numbered and the test strip identified. It is then biscuit-fired.

If two materials A and B are to be used the procedure is as follows: Take two small bowls or cups, label one 'A' the other 'B', and place a given amount (say 100 gms) of material 'A' in cup 'A' and the same quantity of material 'B' into cup 'B'. Add a given amount of water to each cup to make the mixture the consistency of double cream. With a spoon, fill No. 1 of the strip with 'A' and No. 11 with 'B'.

Add 10 gms (10%) of dry material 'B' to cup 'A' and 10 gms (10%) of dry material 'A' to cup 'B'. This means cup 'A' now contains approximately 90% of material 'A' and 10% of material

GLAZING

'B' and vice-versa for cup 'B'. Add water to maintain a creamy mix and mix thoroughly. Fill No. 2 and 10 of the strip. Repeat the procedure of adding 10% of 'B' to cup 'A' and 10% of 'A' to cup 'B' until No. 6 of the strip contains 50% each of 'A' and 'B'. The strip is then fired to the normal glaze temperature prevailing in the pottery. It is useful to carry out such tests with all the main glaze materials, later introducing a third material by making material 'A' a given mixture of two materials.

It is fascinating to see how materials which by themselves remain dry and uninteresting can, when mixed in certain proportions, melt and form the basis of a glaze. It is essential that a notebook be kept so as to record the results of such tests, noting the materials used, the percentage of each material used, the firing temperature and the results that have been achieved.

Initiating new glazes

Until the mid-nineteenth century, glazes were expressed as recipes and not as chemical formulae, and glaze experiments were carried out rather like a cook might experiment with a new recipe; that is by varying the recipe, introducing different materials and checking the results after firing. Careful notes were kept of the recipe, the clay upon which the glaze had been applied, firing conditions and the resultant glaze.

This 'cooks method' is still probably the method of initiating and varying glazes most used by non-industrial potters today. This method works well if the materials being used are understood.

Shoji Hamada as a young man worked in the Kyoto Institute of Ceramics analysing and reproducing early Chinese glazes, and he claims that he has been un-learning such technical knowledge ever since! He now uses a few simple glazes composed of wood-ash, local stone and clay. However, for the student or teacher who wishes to experiment with new glazes, the highly technical formula method will repay study, though outside the scope of this book. Basically the method requires a knowledge of chemistry and chemical properties, coupled with an ability to understand, analyse and assess the formulae likely to produce the glazes required for a particular purpose.

Mixing a glaze

Assuming that a suitable recipe is available (see Chapter Ten) the glaze materials can be weighed out. Always take great care when handling dry ingredients, preferably wearing a dust mask, as prolonged exposure to silica dust can imperil one's health.

It is better to mix sufficient glaze into which can be dipped the largest pieces of work likely to require glazing, particularly large pieces excepted. For a bucket of glaze use 3 kg (7 lbs) total dry weight. For a plastic bin of glaze use total dry weight 10 kg (22 lbs).

It really is unsatisfactory to attempt to glaze when only dregs of glaze are available. Stoneware glaze materials are not very expensive and there is far less wastage if pots can be dipped rather than have glaze poured over them. Pouring usually results in glaze being spilt on the bench or floor, a good reason for also mixing larger bins of earthenware glaze, which is rather more expensive than stoneware glaze.

The dry materials are then mixed with sufficient water to make a liquid of double cream consistency. This is then passed through a phosphor-bronze sieve of 100 mesh using a lawn brush. Some potters insist on using a very fine sieve, such as a 200 mesh, but I must admit to using a 60 mesh for most purposes. Most materials are now finely ground and sieving thoroughly mixes the glaze materials but is seldom required to prevent over-size particles entering the glaze mix. Additional water may be needed to help the last of the materials through the sieve.

Larger potteries mix glazes in a ball-mill but this equipment is not likely to be found in a school pottery or small studio. Although useful, such equipment can be very noisy unless put in solitary confinement in an outside store!

Having mixed the glaze, check it for thickness. The thickness required varies from glaze to glaze. Some glazes are best when thick, others when thin; only experience will indicate which will give the best colour and surface. Earthenware glazes are generally better when applied quite thinly, a litre weighing 1.8 kg (a pint weighing 32 ozs), whereas a lot of stoneware glazes

benefit from a thick coating. The porosity of the biscuit-fired clay will also affect the thickness of the glaze mix required; for this reason it is important always to biscuit-fire to the same temperature if any uniformity of glaze is to be maintained. Most potters use traditional non-scientific ways of judging the thickness of a glaze, such as dipping a scrap of biscuit ware in the glaze and scratching it with the finger nail, and dipping the fingers into the glaze, noting how much glaze clings to them.

Applying the glaze

Pots can be glazed without first being biscuit-fired but this method—whilst it has some advantages, such as the fact that the pots only have to be fired once—is probably unsuitable for use in schools. The pots must be in exactly the right condition for dipping and great certainty and directness are essential. Only the full-time potter is likely to be able to catch pots in the right condition or to have enough practice at dipping such pots. Therefore it is recommended that the pots are glazed after biscuit-firing. Pots can be glazed by spraying, pouring or dipping; the last mentioned is generally the most satisfactory for the school and studio potter although pouring can be useful when glazing large pots and for some types of decorating. Dipping a pot into glaze sounds and appears to be easy. It is easy, but only after considerable practice. Glazing should not be considered as a quick and unimportant process, for while a glaze cannot make a bad pot into a good pot, it can ruin an otherwise good pot.

Glaze dipping

1. Use a thoroughly clean dust-free brush or a damp sponge to remove any dust and trimmings from the biscuit-fired pot, taking care that they do not go into the glaze.
2. If using stoneware, the base of the pot, which will stand on the kiln shelf must be left free of glaze and about 1 cm ($\frac{1}{2}$ in) above the foot should also be left free of glaze in case the glaze runs down during the firing. Experience will indicate if a 1 cm ($\frac{1}{2}$ in) gap is over generous. Failure to leave these areas free of glaze will result in the glaze fusing together the pot and kiln shelf,

so ruining both pot and shelf. Kiln shelves are expensive, and the pot-maker will be disappointed if his pot is spoilt.

When using untried glazes or double-dips (which are described later), it is advisable to leave at least a 5 cm (2 in) unglazed band above the foot or even leave the outside of the pot unglazed.

Leaving the base free of glaze can be achieved in one of three ways:

a) The outside of the pot can be dipped in the glaze, rim first, so leaving the base free of glaze. This is the most straightforward method and to be preferred whenever possible.

b) The base can be glazed with the pot then the unwanted glaze scraped and sponged off.

c) The base can be waxed, the pot glazed and then finally wiped with a clean sponge. The wax mixture most commonly used is candle wax, which can be bought in large slabs, and some ordinary lubricating oil. This mixture is melted in a double saucepan, an old glue pot or a frying pan, care being taken to ensure that the wax does not overheat and catch fire! The wax can be applied by dipping the base or if it has a foot-ring or is too large for dipping, the wax can be applied with a fairly stiff fitch brush as the pot is rotated on a banding wheel.

Do not use an expensive brush, and never a Chinese brush, as the hot wax will melt the glue into which the bristles are set. It is advisable to keep waxing brushes separate from other decorating brushes and clearly mark them. In a school or college situation it is only too easy to have good brushes ruined in the wax pan.

If the wax runs where it is not wanted the only way to remove it is to put the pot in the kiln and biscuit-fire it again. It will not scrape off. Wax resist can be used for decorating; either the hot wax described or a proprietary cold wax-emulsion can be used.

3. Work out the best way to hold the pot for dipping. A firm hold must be maintained, with the minimum contact between fingers and pot. If the pot has a generous foot-ring or part of it is to be left unglazed, it is easy to hold the pot at these points. If the pot has to be held where it is to be glazed it is usually possible to hold the rim, using only one finger on the rim, and im-

mediately the pot is removed from the glaze the finger on the rim can be used to dab on some glaze.

4. Thoroughly stir the glaze that is to be used. This may take five minutes or more if the glaze is not often used. The best way of checking if all the solids have been thoroughly mixed into the suspension is to stir the glaze with the hands. Check that the glaze is of the correct thickness.

5. If the pot to be glazed is basically cylindrical or spherical as opposed to a shallow dish, use a non-drip jug to pour glaze into the pot. Move the pot round until the inside is coated with glaze, taking no longer than about 5 seconds. Pour out the glaze, taking care to avoid dribbles down the outside.

6. Immediately after glazing the inside, dip the pot into the glaze, so as to glaze the outside. Hold the pot in the glaze for approximately 5 seconds, lift it out and shake off any surplus glaze that might cause dribbles. Place the pot on a clean bench.

The way in which the pot is held should have been worked out in Stage 3. A shallow dish can be dipped straight into the glaze, omitting Stage 5.

7. When the pot has dried (this will only take a few minutes except in the

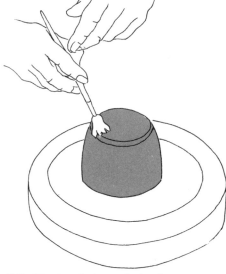

35B: Waxing the base of a bowl.

Fig. 35. Glaze dipping

35A: Dipping a pot rim-first.

35C: Pouring the glaze into a bowl.

35D: Dipping into the glaze.

35E: Wiping the glaze from the base of the bowl.

case of clay/ash glazes which take half an hour or so), the base should be thoroughly wiped, even if wax was used.
8. The pot is now ready for glaze firing. If the pot is to be left for some time before firing, care must be taken to ensure that the glaze surface does not get dusty.

Glazing a teapot

Teapots and coffee pots present particular difficulties when glazing. The shape is quite complicated and great care must be taken to avoid blocking the strainer holes. There are, no doubt, many ways of glazing such pots but the following is one that has proved satisfactory. The waxing of the lid flange and base can be undertaken after the inside has been glazed, so

avoiding the risk of unglazed spots inside the pot, but this will involve wiping off glaze after glazing the inside of the pot.
1. Wax the foot, the lid flange, and all parts of the lid that will be in contact with the pot. This applies to stoneware, in which case the lid is fired in position. For earthenware the lid can be glazed all over and fired separately.
2. Thoroughly stir the glaze to be used.
3. Pour glaze into the pot, using a non-drip jug.
4. Holding finger or thumb over the end of the spout to prevent any flow of glaze,

Fig. 36. Glazing a teapot

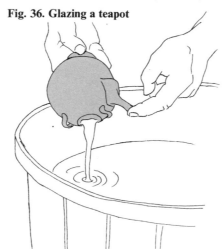

36A: Having poured glaze inside the teapot, it is poured out into the bin.

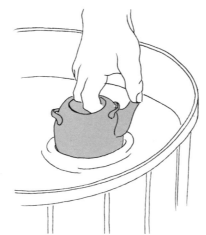

36B: Glazing the outside of a teapot by first dipping the base into the glaze.

rotate the pot so that the inside is fully glazed.
5. Keeping the end of the spout blocked, pour the surplus glaze out through the lid opening, NOT *through the spout. A little will probably pour from the spout when the finger over the spout is released.*
6. When the inside glaze is dry enough to touch, hold the pot with the fingers inside and the thumb over, so blocking, the end of the spout.
7. Dip the pot into the glaze, base first, rock the pot forwards to glaze the spout and back to glaze the handle. Ensure that no glaze enters through the lid opening or spout.
8. Place the pot on a clean bench until the glaze is dry and wipe the waxed areas with a clean, damp sponge.
9. Hold the lid by the waxed area and dip it into the glaze. Hold the lid until it is dry, then wipe the waxed areas with a clean, damp sponge. If the lid is thinner and therefore less absorbent than the body of the pot, either use a thicker glaze mix or dip the lid twice.

Glaze trailing

Glaze can be used rather like slip to give particular decorative effects, under or over an overall glaze. This method of decorating was used by Chinese and Korean potters and is now used by a number of practising potters. Ray Finch at Winchcombe, Gloucestershire, uses glaze trailing in the manner of trailed slip, using a rubber slip trailer. Shoji Hamada, the Japanese potter, pours one glaze over or under an overall glaze, using a large ladle, the results being direct and free.

Thick glaze should be used and applied either with a slip trailer or by pouring. The decoration needs to be directly applied and an over fussy approach is best avoided.

Care must be taken when choosing the glaze to be trailed and tests are best carried out to ensure that the trailed glaze will contrast suitably with the overall glaze of the pot. It should be noted that when one glaze is applied over another there is a tendency for the glazes to become more fluid and move down the pot.

Always apply the second glaze, be it the overall or trailed glaze, when the first glaze is just touch dry. If glaze is applied over another really dry glaze it can cause the glaze to flake off.

Glaze on glaze

This technique, often referred to as double-dipping, can greatly extend the range of glazes available, produce colours and surfaces not obtainable with single glazes and offers an excellent method of decoration.

It can be used for earthenware and stoneware but stoneware offers more scope. The Chinese, Korean and Japanese potters have exploited the interesting colours and decorative effects that this technique offers and a number of practising potters use it very successfully.

The method is quite straightforward. Dip the pot into the first glaze and allow it to become touch dry but not completely dry; this should only take a few minutes. Then dip the pot into the second glaze, taking special care not to chip or spoil the surface of the first glaze. The pot is then left to dry, which will take rather longer than usual, due to the thick coating of glaze.

Before risking a pot it is better to carry out tests on specially prepared test strips or on scraps of biscuit ware. When two glazes are applied there is a tendency for them to become more fluid than when applied separately, so until the results are known, it is advisable to leave a generous unglazed area above the base of the pot.

In addition to an increased colour range, some glazes will crawl when applied over another, so making a pattern reminiscent of small islands.

Wax Resist

An excellent method of decoration is to apply the first glaze, allow it to become touch dry, then brush or pour on a wax pattern. The wax is best applied directly as fussing will cause the first glaze to come off. The pot is then dipped into the second glaze which will be resisted by the wax, so leaving these areas with only the first glaze. This method works well when the Tenmuku glaze is applied, a wax decoration painted on, then the Blue Celadon glaze applied.

Another method of decorating with glaze-on-glaze is to apply the two glazes, then cut and scrape away the second glaze, so making some areas reveal only the first glaze.

Plate 24. Two thrown stoneware plates by Hamada. The example on the left is decorated with brushed iron glaze, that on the right with slip, wax resist and two glazes. The apparently simple decoration involves great skill and control of materials.

MORE ABOUT GLAZES

Glaze faults

Glaze faults can be caused by a faulty clay and in some cases it is easier to modify the clay body. However, as most schools buy a prepared body the only immediate remedy is to modify the glaze. The following are the main faults and suggested remedies.

Crazing

This is the development of a fine network of cracks in the glaze. Crazed ware can be unsightly, unhygienic and permit seepage. In earthenware where the clay body is porous crazing is to be avoided, but in some stoneware glazes crazing can be decorative and so is encouraged. Many examples of Chinese Sung dynasty ware have crazed glazes and such crazing was desired. If crazing is acceptable it is called crackle.

Crazing is caused by the glaze contracting more than the clay body, so leaving tiny cracks between the sections of glaze. To rectify this, the glaze must be adjusted to have a lower rate of expansion and contraction, taking care not to alter the maturing temperature or appearance of the glaze. To effect this adjustment all or some of the following can take place: i) increase the silica; ii) decrease the felspar; iii) decrease any other materials containing soda or potash; iv) increase the boric oxide; v) increase the alumina; vi) decrease any other material with a high coefficient of expansion.

In some cases crazing cannot be eliminated without completely altering colour effects. Turquoise glazes using an alkaline, soda base invariably craze and by reducing the soda the turquoise colour would be lost.

Shivering

This is the opposite of crazing. The clay body contracts more than the glaze, so causing the two to separate and break —that is shiver. If the difference in contraction is not great the glaze will only peel away at the rim or edges of the pot. In order that a glaze does not craze it must be under slight compression, but it is excessive compression that results in shivering.

The remedy for shivering is the opposite of that for crazing. The silica content should be reduced and the high expansion oxides such as soda or potash increased.

Crawling

This occurs during a glaze firing and results in the glaze thickening in some areas and leaving some areas without glaze. It can look like dry mud flats or crazy paving. Whilst generally a glaze fault, carefully controlled crawling can be decorative. A crawled glaze applied over a non-crawled glaze of a different colour can be very pleasing. Shoji Hamada frequently uses glazes that crawl to good effect.

The main causes of crawling are a glaze that is too viscous as opposed to being fluid and a glaze that has a high shrinkage rate when applied to the pot so causing the surface to crack as it dries. If the glaze proves too viscous, small additions of a flux, such as whiting (CaO) or potash (K_2O) can be added to increase its fluidity. If a glaze cracks when applied to the biscuited pot it is usually due to the glaze having a high clay content; ash/clay glazes are particularly prone to cracking before firing. If the fired results prove too unpleasant some of the clay can be replaced by calcined clay or a gum may be added. Subsidiary causes of crawling are dusty biscuited ware, greasy biscuited ware caused by too much handling, and too thick an application of glaze. These causes are very quickly rectified.

Pitting and Pinholing

This results in small, unglazed patches, sometimes little more than pinholes but sometimes like small volcanic craters, which are apparent after glaze firing. They should not be confused with the harmless surface bubbles that sometimes appear on an unfired pot as it is withdrawn from the liquid glaze. The causes of pinholing are usually caused by under- or over-firing the glaze. As the glaze melts it bubbles—as volatile gases escape—before settling down to a smooth surface. If the firing ceases before the glaze has settled down the result will be pinholing. Likewise, if the glaze is overfired so that it boils, the result will be pinholing. The former is rectified by firing to a higher temperature or by reducing the maturing temperature of the glaze by increasing the fluxes. Matt glazes are more prone to pinholing and care must be taken not to alter their surface quality whilst at the same time remedying the pinholing. The second cause, over-firing, is remedied by firing to a lower temperature or by raising the maturing temperature of the glaze by adding a material such as China clay.

If a matt glaze pinholes, it is more likely to be caused by under-firing, but a shiny glaze is more likely to pinhole due to over-firing.

Too thick an application of glaze; too much zinc or rutile in the glaze and too heavy reduction at the early stages of a firing are also possible causes of pinholing.

Bloating

The results of bloating are usually unpleasant, being bulges or bubbles of varying size which develop in the clay during the glaze firing.

The causes are various, but the principal one is the development of small pockets of gas in the clay which are prevented from escaping by the vitrified surface of the clay. The gas can be due to the presence of carbon which combines with oxygen in the clay to form carbon monoxide or dioxide. The carbon is present either due to a rapid biscuit firing which did not enable all carbonaceous matter to be burned out before vitrification, or too early heavy reduction which can cause the formation of carbon in the clay.

The other gas that can be present is water vapour. This is usually due to the biscuited ware being vitrified yet some water penetrates the vitrified surface during glaze dipping. If the subsequent glaze firing is rapid the water vapour is unable to escape before the surface of the clay becomes fully vitrified so that when the clay becomes plastic in the high glaze firing, the water vapour is able to expand and cause bloating.

The remedies for bloating are:

1. Ensure that the biscuit-firing gives ample time for all carbonaceous matter to be burned out and that the kiln vents allow such gases to escape.

2. Do not over-fire the biscuit ware. 980°C–1,000°C is usually a suitable firing temperature.

3. Do not take the glaze-firing up too rapidly and do not introduce a reducing

atmosphere until 1,000°C, and then ensure that the reduction is not too heavy.

4. Associated with the introduction of a reducing atmosphere, ensure that the temperature does not 'stick' around 1,000–1,100°C.

So, basically, bloating can be avoided if care is taken with the firing cycles and when formulating and mixing the clay body.

Dunting and Splitting

Splitting can occur if the body contains too much fine silica and/or if the ware is fired too rapidly between 500°C and 650°C—that is, when the alpha-beta quartz inversion takes place.

Dunting occurs when the kiln is cooling, usually between 700°C and 500°C and results in the pot splitting or cracking. It is caused by too rapid or uneven cooling and is aggravated if the body is high in free quartz and is fine grained and dense.

The remedies for splitting and dunting are:

1. Check the free quartz content of the body and modify it if necessary.

2. Introduce some grog into the body.

3. Take care that the temperature increases steadily when firing and decreases when cooling at a steady rate particularly between 500°C and 700°C.

4. Ensure that no draughts enter the kiln when cooling, particularly between 700°C and 500°C.

Shattering

This is closely allied to shivering and dunting. It can cause pots to break up after glaze-firing, or on occasions this can happen sometime after the pot has been removed from the glaze kiln.

It is caused by the body being too high in free quartz (silica) which can cause the body to have a low contraction rate compared to the glazes applied to it, and which make the body brittle. As the pot cools, the glaze is in such a state of compression that it splits the clay body. Large pots, particularly flat plates which are only glazed on one

side are more prone to shattering as there is no opposing force from the glaze on the outside of the pot.

The remedy is to reduce the amount of free silica in the clay body or even use another body.

Glaze Recipes and Formulas

The following stoneware glazes have proved satisfactory when applied to Potclays' St. Thomas's stoneware body. Most have been used in reducing conditions but comment is given when a glaze has been used in oxidising conditions.

It should be noted that the results obtained from these glazes will vary with the clay body used, variations in materials and variations in firing conditions.

All have been fired to Staffordshire cone 9. 1,280°C.

Ingredients	Parts	
Blue Celadon		
Potash Felspar	60.00	
Quartz	20.00	
Whiting	15.00	
China Clay	5.00	
Red Iron Oxide	1.00	

Crazed but a pleasant blue. Good on porcelain.

Green Celadon		
Talc	10.2	
Potash Felspar	30.0	
Whiting	13.5	
Quartz	32.4	
China Clay	13.9	
Red Iron Oxide	1.0	

Non-crazing. Soft green colour with a typical talc waxy surface.

Dolomite Glaze		
Potash Felspar	48.5	
Dolomite	25.2	
China Clay	22.7	
Whiting	3.6	

A matt cream/white glaze with a satin surface. Pleasant brown and purple flecks.

Tenmuku		
Cornish Stone	71.2	
Cornish Stone	71.2	Firing temp.
Whiting	8.0	1,280°–
Flint	4.5	1,300°C

MORE ABOUT GLAZES

Iron Oxide	6.8
Ball Clay	7.0
Bentonite	2.0

Non-crazing. A red/brown glaze breaking to black when applied thickly. A shiny wax-like surface.

Semi-shiny Brown

Soda Felspar	25
Dolomite	15
China Clay	25
Bone Ash	10
Quartz	25
Red Iron	10

A semi-shiny glaze with colour variation of red, brown and black. A useful glaze in oxidising conditions.

Talc White

Talc	16.68
Potash Felspar	27.50
Whiting	12.37
China Clay	13.74
Flint	29.70

A semi-shiny glaze. Non-crazing, even on porcelain. Pleasant waxy surface. Blue/white in reduction, creamy white in oxidation.

Yellow Ash

Dry red clay	48.9
Wood Ash (soft)	48.9
Bentonite	2.0

A semi-matt glaze. Yellow to green in colour. Useful in oxidation and reduction. The wood ash used is primarily from soft woods.

Dry Blue Ash

Wood Ash (soft)	33.0
China Clay	33.0
Felspar Potash	33.0
Cobalt Oxide	0.5

A dry blue glaze, breaking to green where thin. Useful in oxidation and reduction.

The wood ash used is primarily from soft woods.

Raku Glaze

High Alkaline Fritt	85.0
Whiting	5.0
China Clay	10.0

Firing temp. 750°C–850°C.
A clear, shiny glaze to which colouring and opacifying oxides can be added. 2% copper oxide gives turquoise. 2% manganese plus 0.25% cobalt gives a dark purple. 5% tin oxide gives an opaque white. All are affected by reduction.

Testing clay bodies and glazes

There are two approaches to clay- and glaze-making and testing—the 'cook's approach' and a highly technical scientific analytical approach.

The 'cook's approach' takes a known and proven recipe as a starting point, and modifications are made to it, remembering and noting all variations. This method works well if the behaviour of the various materials is known and it is possible to fire a reasonable number of tests. It is hardly economic to fire a kiln just for tests.

The analytical method is to formulate the clay and glazes using chemical analysis of the materials used and working within recommended limits for these materials. This method requires an understanding of both chemistry and mathematics, and is really outside the scope of this book. Its chief advantage is that serious errors and disappointments are less likely, an intimate knowledge of the materials is gradually built-up, and if a particular material becomes difficult to obtain, it is possible to satisfy the formula using different materials.

It must be admitted, however, that few studio potters regularly use clay and glaze formulae when experimenting. They tend to use the 'cook's approach' for obvious reasons.

The 'cook's approach' to glaze experiments

This approach to glazes is similar to that of a cook who takes a basic cake recipe, then varies it to alter the flavour or texture of the cake, recording the new recipe for future use.

If the line-blend experiments discussed in Chapter 4 have been undertaken, and the information given in Chapter 2 and Appendix 1 on glaze materials is referred to, an understanding of the effects of the different materials on each other will have been established.

For earthenware glazes a basic frit, firing at the required temperature, is a good starting point. To this frit may be added other materials. For stoneware take a simple recipe such as:

Potash felspar	80
Whiting	15
China clay	5

or an established recipe which shows promise.

Weigh out a given amount, 200 gms (7–8 oz) total weight is a useful quantity for tests, making approximately 0.2 litres (⅓ pint) of liquid glaze. Sieve the glaze and apply to a test strip of biscuited clay approximately 5 cm × 3 cm (2 in × 1¼ in) or preferably to the inside of a small test bowl. Such test bowls can be thrown or pinched out, and 2 cm (¾ in) is a useful diameter. They provide a better indication of the behaviour of a glaze on a curved surface. Then, if a glaze proves very fluid it merely pools in the bottom of the bowl instead of spoiling a kiln shelf.

Number the test with iron or manganese oxide and record it in a notebook. The record should give the clay used, glaze recipe, firing type, firing temperature and the result.

To the basic glaze add the fourth ingredient: 1%–10% can be added depending on the material, sieve and if necessary add more water so that the glaze is of single cream consistency. Apply to a test bowl or strip, numbering and recording the test.

Repeat this procedure at 1% or 2% intervals until sufficient tests have been undertaken. The total useful addition can be gauged from previous experience and the notes on the various materials in Chapter 2 and Appendix 1.

Such tests may be carried out to alter the surface of a glaze from shiny to matt, to make a transparent glaze opaque, to make a crazing glaze fit the clay body without crazing or to colour the glaze.

When the tests have been fired assess the results and record them under each of the listed glaze tests. It is as well to delete those recipes which show little promise and pursue further tests with those that look hopeful. All good glazes involve a certain amount of luck or intuition but careful records help in obtaining such lucky breaks!

As an understanding of the materials is acquired and some basic glaze recipes become established, the tests will become more straightforward and useful.

DECORATION

Whether to decorate a pot and by which method, or to leave it to rely on its form and glaze for beauty is always a difficult problem.

For the past three decades or so decoration has been out of fashion—particularly decoration that is not a direct result of the making process. There seems to be two principal reasons for this lack of decoration. A conscious rejection of the highly decorated work that the pottery industry was producing in vast quantities in the Victorian era (and continued to produce well into the 20th century), and a desire to return to the simpler straightforward work of the country potters.

The second reason is the fact that many of our recent potters who excel as pot-makers and are very competent throwers, have not had any graphic training or the time in which to become equally competent decorators. There are obvious exceptions to this general trend—for example David Leach, who decorates by applying metal oxides such as iron and cobalt with a Chinese brush; Alan Caiger-Smith, who applies metal lustres to a Majolica glaze; Michael Casson, who also uses brushed oxides as well as brushing on slips and dry ash glazes and Henry Hammond, who uses painted pigment with such delicacy.

In the last few years more potters have started to decorate their pots, even if somewhat tentatively. However, when it is noted that until the 1940's very few art schools were able to teach their students to be competent throwers due to the fact that there just were not any teachers available who could throw, the general technical standard of pottery has greatly improved. Perhaps in a few years time more potters will have the technical ability to decorate, as well as discernment and restraint. Decoration can be placed under various headings according to the method of application.

Modelled Decoration

This can take the form of direct modelling onto the pot or low-relief ornament which is first modelled then applied to the pot; this is known as 'sprigging'.

CHAPTER 11

Direct modelling can be applied as feet, knobs or handles. Such modelling has been used by most cultures, including the Chinese, Greek, Roman, Nigerian, Inca and Medieval English. In many cases it was applied for reasons of use; for example, the small loop handles applied to the belly of a Chinese Sung dynasty pot were originally for threading a rope to assist in carrying the pot. The handles applied to jugs and the knobs applied to lids continue to be essentially for use, although they fulfil the secondary yet important role of being decorative. Direct modelling has also been used purely for decorative purposes, such as the modelled faces on some Medieval English jugs and the swirling coil decoration used on some Nigerian pots.

A step-by-step description of how to model is hardly appropriate but care should be taken to ensure that the pot is damp enough to accept additions and that none of the modelling is more than about 2.5 cm (1 in) square in section unless grogged clay is being used. Modelling over 2.5 cm (1 in) square should be hollowed to avoid the danger of breakage during firing. Sprigging permits more elaborate and delicate designs to be applied. This method was used by the Romans, Medieval potters, the German salt-glaze potters and Josiah Wedgwood. The latter's work is still produced and consists of delicate white decoration on a blue or green ground. Such decoration was ideal when first produced—the period of the architect and interior designer Robert Adam who used such delicate relief decoration in his house interiors.

The method involves the use of shallow moulds made from wood, plaster, or more commonly, biscuited clay. The mould is prepared, taking care not to have any under-cuts that will prevent clay from coming away freely. The moulds should be quite small, not more than about 5 cm (2 in) across. Clay is pressed into the mould, then by pressing a flat blade onto the clay the relief is lifted from the mould.

It can either be kept damp while more reliefs are made, or placed directly onto the pot, which should be just damp enough for the sprig to stick without using slip.

The advantage of sprigging is that the surface of the pot is not disturbed and

DECORATION

Plate 25. British studio pottery: an attractive stoneware jar by Katherine Pleydell-Bouverie.

Plate 26. Korean porcelain pot of the Yi dynasty, 17th–18th centuries A.D. It was thrown, and then the sides cut. Painted with copper-red decoration.

impressions can be made when the pot has stiffened but is still quite soft. If it is a slab pot it is better to cut out all the slabs and decorate them before assembly. This will allow the impressions to be made before the clay becomes too stiff. Similar objects can be used to decorate tiles, wall panels and small panels that can be attached to a pot, rather like sprigging.

Care must be taken when using stamps and 'found objects' not to use too many different objects or to over-decorate, otherwise the result will be muddled and the pot will not be enhanced. Always experiment on a slice of clay before committing the pot.

Another method of impressing decoration is to use a roulette, a tool of great antiquity, much favoured by the Romans. It consists of a carved cylinder

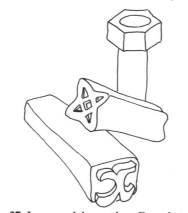

Fig. 37. Impressed decoration. Carved stamps, nuts and bolts, and other similar objects may be used.

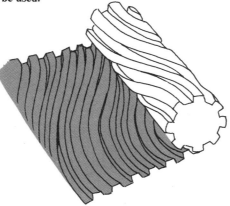

Fig. 38. Roulette—a carved cylinder used for impressing a repeated pattern.

the same motif can be repeated. The danger is that the decoration can become fussy and lifeless, even though great skill might be involved. Such a criticism could be levelled at much of the sprig-decorated wares produced by industrial potteries.

Cut decoration
Pots can be cut or planed to give facets. This can be done with a wire as soon as the pot is thrown, or when it is leather-hard. Care must be taken to allow adequate thickness in the wall of the pot.

Another means of faceting the pot is to beat it when leather-hard.

Impressed Decoration
This method of decoration has been used in various forms by most cultures, ranging from the basket-like impressions of Neolithic pots to the decorated attachments of English 18th century creamware. In recent years it has proved a popular method of decoration for pots and for wall panels.

The techniques used are quite simple and the ideal of close integration between pot and decoration is combined with a spontaneous and direct approach. The impressions can be pressed into the soft clay in a number of different ways; the simplest being to press in 'found objects'. The objects could include: nuts and bolts, cog-wheels, pieces of wood, screw-heads, rolled string, pebbles, sea shells, cotton reels, stiff brushes and clay stamps. If the pot has been coiled or thrown the

of clay, plaster, wood or metal which can be rolled along the surface of the pot to impress a repeated pattern. A more sophisticated roulette is one where the roller is drilled in the centre, a spindle inserted and mounted on a handle—rather like a pastry wheel. The wheels can be shaped for concave or convex surfaces and can, by carving the appropriate letters, be used to impress the potter's name.

The roulette should be used on soft, even freshly-thrown clay. Slab pots are best decorated before assembly.

Incised Decoration (Sgraffito)
What are almost certainly some of the most beautiful pots ever made have been enhanced by the use of incised decoration. The pots are those of the Chinese T'ang and Sung dynasties which were thrown in white porcellaneous clay then incised with a decoration of simple flowers. By using thick celadon glaze apparent depth has been given to the incising without disturbing the surface of the glaze.

So, one type of incised decoration involves the cutting away of fine lines when the clay is leather-hard. A sharpened piece of bamboo is probably the best tool for this purpose. Another method is to apply slip to the partially dry pot then incise through the slip to the clay body. It is necessary to ensure that the clay is firm enough to permit a clean cut without a burr being left along the edges of the cut. If the clay is too dry it will be found difficult to cut.

Plate 27. Stoneware jar of the northern Sung dynasty, China, 11th–12th centuries A.D. Thrown, it has incised decoration, and olive green celadon glaze.

Plate 28. An example of Japanese Seto ware from 13th–14th centuries A.D. Thrown, it has incised decoration with brown glaze.

Pigments in the form of metal oxides can be brushed onto the leather-hard pot and an incised decoration cut, so giving a contrast between the pigment and the clay body.

A more difficult form of incised decoration but one that can be very effective is to incise through unfired glaze, so leaving a contrast of glazed and unglazed lines. This method was used to great effect by the potters of China during the Sung dynasty. Most Chinese pots were glazed before being fired, and then once fired. Glaze is easier to incise when on an unfired pot as the risk of the glaze flaking off is reduced. It is possible to incise through a glaze on a biscuit-fired pot if a non-flaking glaze is chosen, but it is still very difficult.

Fluting

Fluting can be included under the heading of incised decoration, although rather more clay is removed by fluting than by the other methods of incising. The greatest exponents of fluting were the potters of the Chinese Sung Dynasty —such decoration responding to celadon glazes in the same way as their finer incised decoration. Some twentieth century potters, notably Bernard Leach and David Leach, have revived this type of decoration which can either be cut with a metal tool or a piece of cut bamboo. The metal tool is used like a woodworker's plane and gives the fluting a slightly-rounded section. The bamboo tool is cut to a chisel end, the hard outer layer being the blade, and is drawn in an arc across the pot, which is

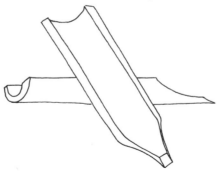

Fig. 39. A bamboo fluting tool. It is held like a pencil, the hard outer layer of the bamboo being the cutting edge.

held horizontally; with practice this gives crisp, hard-edged fluting. Such crisp fluting is very effective when a semi-matt white glaze is used.

Slip Decoration

Slip decoration is usually associated with earthenware but it can be used very effectively with stoneware, provided care is taken to ensure that the slips used are effective at the higher temperature required for stoneware.

Slip can be used in many ways as a means of decorating and it can greatly increase the range of colours obtainable from both earthenware and stoneware glazes. Slip is simply a sieved liquid clay, the colour of which can vary, with the type of clay used, from red earthenware to white ball clay. The range of colours can be extended by mixing slips and by adding metal oxides. The colour will vary with the firing temperature and the glaze, if any, that is applied.

Some basic slips are:

(i)	Ball clay 100%	creamy white
(ii)	Buff clay body 100%	creamy white
(iii)	China clay 50% Ball clay 50%	white

For stoneware add up to 25% of China clay to prevent the slip becoming part of the glaze melt.

(iv)	Red clay body 100%	Red/brown in earthenware Dark brown in stoneware
(v)	Red clay body 47%	A black slip breaking to
	Buff clay body 47%	dark blue through
	Manganese 5%	some stone-
	Cobalt 1%	ware glazes

Slips should be sieved through a 60-mesh sieve and be approximately the consistency of double cream. Experience will indicate the best consistency for each slip and each process. Many other slips can be mixed, particularly if colouring oxides are added to a basic white slip. Always remember that the clay body, the slip and any glaze that is applied over it are interdependent; the slip and the body must have a similar shrinkage rate if the slip is to adhere and the slip will influence the colour of the glaze and vice-versa.

USING SLIPS

Dipping

The simplest method of slip decoration is to dip a leather-hard pot into slip. Care should be taken to ensure that the pot is not too wet or too dry; the former will not take up sufficient slip and will cause the pot to collapse, the second will probably crack.

This simple dipping method can be extended by dipping the pot into various slips, holding it at different angles to make patterns with slip and increasing the range of colours obtained by overlapping the slips.

Wax Resist

The wax is painted onto the leather-hard

DECORATION

pot where the body colour is to be retained. The wax can be painted as simple bands or in a representational manner or in a free way using the possibilities offered by brush strokes. The pot is then dipped or brushed with slip.

The wax used can be of two types: (a) A wax emulsion, available from potters' merchants, or (b) a mixture of paraffin wax and lubricating oil. The second type is more often used and the thickness can be varied by adding more oil. The thicker the medium that has to be resisted, the thicker the wax required. The mixture of wax and oil has to be melted over a low heat until it begins to smoke. Take care it does not catch fire or spill!

Brushed Slip

This method of decoration has been used by most cultures, including the Chinese and our own. Care should be taken when brushing slip to ensure that ample slip is applied. The slip needs to be rather thicker than would be suitable for dipping. A large Chinese brush or a glazing mop, which will hold plenty of slip, are usually the most suitable brushes. The brush can be used in a graphic way or just as an alternative to dipping the pot into slip.

Paper stencils can be cut from thin paper (newspaper is ideal), moistened to stick it to the pot and slip brushed on. When the slip has dried a little the paper stencil should be peeled away. This method of decoration is more suited to slab pots and shallow dishes, although thin stencils can be persuaded to stick to large thrown pots if care is taken to prevent the paper creasing.

Hakeme is a type of brushed slip which originated in Korea and was later introduced to Japan by Korean potters in the 15th century. A possible reason for its introduction is that white clays are, compared with red clays, rare, with the result that many potters, particularly in poor countries such as Korea, used white slip with caution. Far less slip is used if it is brushed on than when a pot is dipped into slip. Whether Korean potters first brushed on slips for such economic reasons, as opposed to aesthetic reasons, is obscure. Whatever the reason, the results are in many cases quietly beautiful.

Shoji Hamada is one of the few modern potters to use the Hakeme technique successfully, some of his pots using Hakeme surely ranking as among the most notable of the 20th century.

The Hakeme technique is, in itself, quite simple. Thick white slip is brushed onto the leather-hard pot with a very coarse brush.

Inlaying Slip

This method of decoration is little-practised today but is perhaps due for a revival. The probable reason for this lack of popularity is the number of processes involved in its execution and hence the time involved. The superb tiles which were used in many medieval churches, and can still be found in the less-frequented and less-worn parts of such churches, are fine examples of the bold use of slip inlay. The tiles were made by pressing the clay into a wooden die which produced a tile with a sunken pattern. When leather-hard the pattern was filled with a slip of another colour — usually a red tile was filled with white slip — and when the inlay became leather-hard the tile was scraped flat, revealing a clean, sharp pattern. When dry the tiles were dusted with galena and fired to a low earthenware temperature. The tiles were 2 cm–2.5 cm ($\frac{3}{4}$–1 in) thick and the slip between 3 mm–6 mm ($\frac{1}{8}$ in–$\frac{1}{4}$ in) thick, hence their long life.

Some medieval pots were inlaid with slip but it was not frequently used on pots. The great practitioners of inlaid slip on pots were the Koreans of the Koryo Dynasty (918–1392 A.D.). The decoration was first cut into the leather-hard pot; slips of contrasting colours were basted into the cuts; when the slip became leather-hard it was scraped down to reveal a sharp pattern, often of amazing delicacy and detail. The decoration was sometimes based on plant forms and sometimes almost geometric, particularly on the small-lidded boxes. A dull green celadon glaze was usually applied. It is interesting that this technique remained almost peculiar to Korea and was not much used in China, despite being admired by members of the Chinese Sung court.

The technique used for slip inlay has already been mentioned. An impression is either stamped or cut into the clay and filled with a slip that will contrast

Plate 30. English earthenware 'tyg', A.D. 1636. Thrown in red clay with white slip decoration and a honey-coloured lead glaze. A tyg was a cup with three or more handles.

Plate 29. English Staffordshire earthenware c. 1675. The slip decoration in red clay on this dish is intended to depict King Charles II hiding in the oak tree.

Plate 31. Bernard Leach made this earthenware dish in 1923—studio pottery at its best.

with the clay body. The main difficulties that arise, apart from skill of cutting the decoration, are matching the shrinkage rate of the slip to that of the clay body and the fact that the slip soaks back into the pot as it dries, so making more than one infilling necessary. If the slip does not contract as much as the body during drying and firing it can cause the body to split; this fault can be rectified by adding some very plastic clay with a high shrinkage rate, to the slip. If the slip contracts more than the body, and so starts to peel away from the body, a clay with a low shrinkage rate, such as China clay, should be added to the slip. A clear glaze should be applied so as to reveal the decoration; this applies to stoneware and earthenware.

Slip trailing

Slip had been used in England during the Roman occupation but such refinements departed with the Romans and slip was rarely used until the 14th century, when some fine examples of brushed slip decoration were produced. It was during the 17th and 18th centuries that English slip-ware really flourished; slip-ware should not be confused with slip-casting which is primarily an industrial technique for making pots and is not discussed in this book. At this time the well-known slip-ware potters, Thomas Toft and Ralph Simpson, were producing their large commemorative plates with exuberant slip-trailed decoration. Despite the industrialisation of the pottery industry, slip-ware continued to be produced by a few country potters until the 1920's and 1930's—the last country potters sadly gave up the struggle to keep going just before the pottery revival that started in the 1940's and is, thankfully, still with us.

Slip trailing can be likened to icing a cake—a basic ground is applied, the decoration is piped on. Due to the fluid quality of slip, it is easier to use on a shallow dish than on a pot, but pots should not be excluded, for with practice they can be decorated very effectively. Press-moulded dishes are best decorated before the slice of clay is pressed over the mould—ensuring that the slip is not tacky but the slice is still damp enough to press over the mould without cracking.

The basic method is to dip one side of

Fig. 40. Slip decorating using a rubber slip-trailer to decorate a small bowl. The bowl should be leather-hard and the slip the consistency of double cream.

a slice or one surface of a pot, inside or outside, with slip, so giving a smooth ground. The clay should be soft when dipped, but not wet from throwing. Only one surface is slipped to avoid the pot becoming too wet and heavy. That would cause it to collapse.

Slip of a contrasting colour and a little thicker than that used for dipping is poured or sucked into a trailer—usually a rubber bulb with a glass or plastic nozzle. Then, by careful control of the slip-trailer, an even line of slip can be drawn across the pot or slice of clay, care being taken not to scrape the slip ground with the trailer nozzle. The best slip-trailing is fluid, direct and sympathetic to the form being decorated. It can become highly complex, a demonstration of the potter's skill, rather like the large Toft plates, with their trellis work in two colours, figures and delicate blobs. If the slip is inclined to stand up too much it can be thinned, or the pot carefully jolted, so that the trailing sinks into the slip ground.

An even more direct method of slip-trailing is to use a ladle with a small hole. This method does not permit any detailed work but requires great directness and skill to be effective. Hamada has produced some fine work using this technique.

Combing

This is an extension of slip-trailing, although it is frequently used when only the ground slip has been applied. While the slip is still wet, a piece of stiff leather or wood with rounded teeth is drawn through the slip, making straight or flowing lines. The fingers can be used in place of the leather or wood. It is essential to be direct and no attempt

DECORATION

to alter the decoration should be made as this will only make the decoration messy.

Feathering

This also follows on from slip-trailing and was much favoured by country potters for decorating large moulded dishes. Most museums that have a section dealing with domestic ware of the 18th and 19th centuries have good examples of feather combing.

As with slip-trailing, a slice of clay is placed on a board and a slip ground is poured over it—usually a red slip. A few minutes later, while the ground is still wet, a series of parallel lines are trailed in white slip. The board is then jolted so that the two slips form a smooth surface. Then a feather, which has been sharpened to a long fine point, is drawn across the clay, so dragging one slip out into the other with great delicacy. Variations on this basic method are to use more than one colour of slip to trail the lines and to draw the feather across the trailing in alternate directions. If a feather is not available, a bristle plucked from a hand broom makes a suitable alternative.

When the slip has ceased to be tacky the decorated slabs can be pressed over a mould and trimmed, either to a flat rim or a scalloped edge. The latter was frequently favoured by country potters.

Thrown pots can also be decorated by feather combing, but this requires considerable dexterity and much practice. It is magic to watch a skilled potter decorating in this way.

Marbling

This is yet another variation of slip-trailing. It can be used as a rescue operation if the slip-trailing or feathering has become messy, but this is not to be encouraged! The bowl or slab of clay is violently shaken and twisted while the slip is still wet, so making the various slips run into each other and producing a pattern a little like marble or the contour lines on a map. A more definite way of producing marbled decoration is to apply the first slip on the inside of a bowl or on a slice of clay, then make a series of blobs around the edge with a slip of a different colour. The bowl or slice is then shaken or twisted until a marbled effect is achieved. Care should be taken not to attempt to make the pattern too complicated by shaking and twisting as the slips will mix together into a muddy mess.

The methods of slip decorating described can be varied and combined in numerous ways. It is better to practise on a slice of clay from which the slip can be wiped and a fresh start made, rather than ruin pots with poor decoration.

Painting with pigments

Painting with pigments was one of the most widely used methods of decoration employed in the West from the 9th century to the Industrial Revolution of the early 18th century. It was certainly the most widely used method of decorating in China from the T'ang dynasty

Plate 32. Tenmoku on red slip, a superb piece made by Michael Casson in 1973.

Plate 33. Tz'u chou stoneware of the Chinese Sung dynasty, A.D. 960–1279. Thrown with semi-matt glaze and brushed iron decoration.

Plate 34. Thrown winter-shape tea-bowl by Shoji Hamada. Stoneware with iron decoration.

Plate 35. Porcelain pot of the Korean Yi dynasty, 17th or 18th century. Thrown, with painted decoration.

(618–906 A.D.) to the end of the Ching dynasty (1912 A.D.). Incised decoration was also very widely used, particularly during the earlier period. These facts can be confirmed by glancing at any collection of European pottery made before the early 18th century and a comprehensive collection of Chinese pottery.

European brushwork was killed by industrialisation, which introduced the use of transfers and the application of overglaze enamels, which were diluted with oil instead of water and applied to an already glazed surface. The small amount of hand painting which continued in the pottery factories was, and continues to be fussy, uninspired and owes little to its method of application.

A study of the brushwork executed by the Moors in Spain, the early Delft potters in Holland and the Chinese of the Sung dynasty illustrate the way in which brushed decoration can enhance a pot.

It would require a complete book to describe and illustrate the brush strokes and colours that can be used to decorate. The Chinese prepared such manuals, illustrating sixty or more ways of painting leaves and so on, but it is outside the scope of this book and much can be learned by using different brushes without using a step-by-step commentary.

One reason why many potters do not use brush decoration (in addition to the fact that it is out of fashion), is that they have devoted all their time to becoming competent pot-makers and have not had the time or training to become experts with a brush. It should be remembered that the Chinese potters established a system of division of labour so that each process in making a pot was carried out or supervised by a specialist. It is thought that many of the much-admired Sung dynasty pots were decorated by teenage boys, whose thoughts might well have been on more mundane things than careful brushwork. This could be responsible for the superbly-free, even light-hearted results. Representational patterns are probably best avoided, although most traditional patterns have a descriptive, literary or symbolic origin. Constant repetition of the same pattern over a long period

Fig. 41. A selection of brushes. From the top: a square liner, a cut-liner, a Chinese brush and a glaze mop.

of time has resulted in a loss of the representational element and in an increasing abstract rhythm which is often more beautiful and suitable. The best brushwork is not tight and mechanically accurate but is alive, free and yet controlled.

The only way of striving toward such a goal is to have a selection of brushes of different sizes—liners, Chinese, soft mops and any other type of brush that holds promise. In order that not too many pots are ruined, the brushes can be tried out on paper, using fairly liquid poster paint. Various strokes and combinations of strokes can be tried with each brush, until the possibilities of each brush are revealed. Allow the brush to do the work—do not attempt to make a brush paint a line for which it is not suited. Painting on a flat surface with paint is not the same as painting on a pot with metal oxides, but it will give some idea of what can be achieved, and provides a means of practice.

Under-glaze painting

As the name implies, the decoration is painted onto the pot before it is dipped into the glaze. It can be done while the pot is green or after biscuit firing. In many ways, it is better to paint on the slightly damp unfired clay, for it is a nice surface upon which to paint. Some colours, notably blue,

benefit from blending with the clay and the subsequent biscuit firing fixes the colours. This prevents them from running during the glazing process and glaze firing.

The colouring oxides only need to be mixed with water and ground on a glazed tile with a palette knife before application. The main disadvantage of painting on the raw pot should be considered. The pot is rather fragile for handling. Far more care must be taken when packing the biscuit kiln so as to avoid scraping the decoration or smudging it, or transferring colour from one pot to another and particularly in schools there is the danger of inquisitive fingers smudging the decoration before it is biscuit-fired.

The surface of a biscuit-fired pot is not as smooth and receptive to the brush as the unfired clay but it does have advantages. Less time and kiln space is needed for the biscuit-firing, the pot is stronger and can withstand more handling. The pot is decorated then dipped into glaze, so preventing smudging by inquisitive fingers. The disadvantages are the danger of the colour running during firing and a tendency for some of the colour to come off during glazing. Both of these disadvantages can, to a large extent, be overcome by mixing the colouring oxide with some China clay and talc when grinding it ready for painting. The clay and talc make the colouring oxide less fluid when glaze fired, make it harder and less powdery when it is being dipped into the glaze, and enables the colour to be used as a smooth medium, which aids painting. The proportion of china clay, talc and colouring oxide will vary, depending on the strength of the colouring oxide being used and the colour required. In stoneware, cobalt oxide, the strongest of the colouring oxides, will give a strong blue when used in the ratio of 1 part cobalt, 4 parts china clay, 4 parts talc. Whereas iron oxide will give a yellow/brown when used in the ratio of 1 part iron oxide, 1 part china clay, 1 part talc. The colour obtained varies considerably with the glaze used and the type of firing. The talc also affects the colour, cobalt in particular. Some potters use gum arabic or gum of tragacanth.

DECORATION

To sum up the advantages and disadvantages of applying brush decoration to fired or unfired pots, it is probably better for the individual potter who has control of all the processes in a pottery to paint onto the unfired pot, whereas in a school it is better to paint on the biscuited ware.

When the decoration is to be painted sufficient colour should be ground to complete the pot, or series of pots, if some uniformity of colour is to be achieved—see list of colouring oxides which follow later in this chapter.

Faint pencil lines can be drawn on the pot as guides for painting but do NOT draw in detail and then fill in with paint, as though you were 'painting by numbers'. Keep the guide lines practically invisible. The pot can be held in the hand or placed on a banding wheel—it depends very much on the shape and size of the pot to be decorated. The brush is then loaded with colour and the decoration executed.

Touching-up the decoration should be avoided, for painting the same area twice will add more oxide and so alter the colour. It is rather like water colour painting, not oil painting where a second or third application of paint will obscure that which it covers. It is the fact that the amount of colouring oxide applied will greatly alter the colour obtained, together with the glaze that is applied, that makes any definite prediction of results quite impossible. Unlike oil paint or household emulsion paint, where a particular colour can be chosen and applied, the results of under-glaze painting can only be approximated even after considerable experience of the quantities to use, thickness of application, glazes, and firing conditions. Surely it is this element of chance and hope that contributes to the thrill of pottery.

If the decorating has been applied to an unfired pot it should be fired as soon as it is dry. If the pot is already biscuited it should be glazed as soon as the colour is dry. In both cases, care should be taken to handle the pots as little as possible so as to avoid smudging the decoration.

Overglaze painting

This involves painting with colouring oxides onto unfired glaze. It should not be confused with on-glaze painting which refers to painting onto fired glaze with enamels.

Overglaze painting was used to decorate Italian Majolica, Delft, and wares of a similar kind. Such wares were inspired by the brush-decorated white stoneware and porcelain that had been imported into the Western world from China. The technique of making porcelain or white stoneware had not been discovered in Europe, so pots of red or buff clay were glazed with a white opaque glaze and decorated before the glaze firing. This technique has remained in use ever since, although very few potters now use it, despite a revival in the 1950's. Its recent decline is due to a number of factors—the popularity of stoneware; the relatively high failure rate compared to stoneware; the expense of the glaze ingredient, tin oxide in particular; the time and skill involved in brush decoration.

The basic method for Majolica ware is to make the pots from a clay with a fairly high shrinkage rate, so that the glaze can be craze-free, and which starts to fuse at 1,000°C, so becoming fairly strong and less likely to chip. Gault clay—high in calcium—was traditionally used but as this is difficult to obtain in some countries alternatives—such as Fremington clay in England—have to be used.

After biscuiting, a tin glaze is applied. Any earthenware glaze firing at about 1,060°C plus 10–12% tin oxide will suffice but it is better to use a glaze with a low alumina and low clay content. The former will render the glaze more stable and the second will give the glaze a low-drying shrinkage and so prevent cracking in the glaze, which could lead to crawling. Cornish stone assists opacity. Lead glazes tend to be visually softer than those using a lead/borax frit, but the latter is probably a safer base for a glaze in these days of poisoning scares.

When the glaze is almost dry—that is, touch dry but not bone dry—the colours may be painted on. So as to avoid disturbing the glaze surface the brush must be soft, hold a large amount of colour and be used directly.

The oxides most commonly used, alone or in combination, are iron, cobalt, copper, manganese, antimonate of lead and vanadium. The oxides can be mixed before application or superimposed when decorating. The oxides are best mixed with water and ground on a tile or piece of plate glass with a palette knife—they should be used thinly. Tin glaze does not run, so all unevenness tends to show. Once the decorating has been completed, the pot should be fired as soon as possible, to avoid the danger of chipping.

Lustres can also be applied to a tin glaze. They were used in the Middle East from the 9th century and it remained a dominantly Middle Eastern technique, although the Moors introduced it into Spain and it had a brief spell of popularity in Europe during the 19th and early 20th centuries. Unfortunately potteries, such as Leeds and Sunderland in England, used lustres to cover a pot completely and so make it appear to be made of silver or gold. This has given lustre a bad name. Painted with skill and restraint, lustre decoration can be excellent.

The lustres are applied to a fired tin glaze which will soften at 650°C.

Suitable lustres are:

Copper Carbonate	*30 parts*
Red Ochre	*70 parts*
Silver Sulphide	*30*
Red Ochre	*70*

The ochre distributes the metal evenly and prevents volatilisation. The oxide and ochre are mixed in vinegar so that the smaller particles are dissolved and a more even distribution is achieved. No gum is used. The pot is then refired in a very dry kiln as any steam will cause the lustre to dribble. The kiln is fired to 650°C in oxidising condition, then strongly reduced for about an hour—by which time the temperature should be about 700°C. Until the behaviour of the lustres on a particular glaze is known it is better to have test rings—small loops of clay which have been glazed and decorated—which can be withdrawn from the kiln to judge whether the pots are fired. The ochre, which will remain a surface powder after firing, is then brushed off and the lustre polished. Further reading is recommended before trying out painted lustre.

On-glaze decoration (Enamels)

This type of decoration is now seldom used by studio potters, although some of the recent work by students at colleges of art indicate that it might be due for a come-back. It is unfortunately associated with the highly ornate—some would say tasteless—bone china wares of the pottery industry. Used with discretion, it can add welcome colour to the otherwise restrained tones of reduced stoneware. Hamada uses bright, child-like colours most effectively.

Enamels can be mixed by using a lead and quartz base in the proportion of lead 40%: quartz 60%. To this colouring oxides are added. It is, however, very difficult to mix good reds and yellows and thus it is probably better to buy enamels from the potters' merchants, who also sell a turpentine medium with which to mix the enamels.

After mixing on a tile with a palette knife the enamels are painted onto the glaze-fired pot, allowed to dry and fired in a well-ventilated kiln to the temperature recommended by the enamel supplier, usually between 700°C and 800°C.

Colouring pigments

The colouring pigments used in pottery are all derived from metals, be they common metals such as iron and copper or less familiar metals such as uranium. It is these pigments that are responsible

Plate 36. Peruvian water pot. Coiled and unglazed, with red, black and white slip decoration.

for the colour of natural rocks. Iron being the most plentiful, is responsible for much of the colour apparent in our landscape, be it the dark red/browns of the earth or the yellow of clay.

Iron responds well to different glazes, firing temperature and firing atmosphere. It can give soft blues, a variety of greens ranging from gentle soft hues to deep dark shades; yellows ranging from a pale honey to yellow/brown; and browns ranging from dark red to black. The Chinese Sung potters rarely used any other pigment in addition to iron and it remains the most useful colouring oxide although we can now choose from a great variety supplied by the potters' merchants.

It is quite pointless having a bag of everything listed because (a) some oxides having very limited use due to a restricted firing range, (b) danger from poisoning and (c) high cost. Always check that an oxide is suited to the firing temperature being used. It is better to make good use of a restricted palette—and get to know how to use a few colours—than have numerous colours that are not understood or used to advantage.

The following lists some of the more useful colouring oxides:

Antimonate of lead

Approximately $3PbO\ Sb_2O_3$

The 'Naples Yellow' of the paint box. A useful yellow for earthenware. It can be added to a clear, lead glaze in quantities up to 10% and when used as a pigment is best mixed with a soft lead frit in the proportion 1:1. **This substance is highly poisonous, so its use must be restricted.**

Chromium Oxide Cr_2O_3

The green type of this oxide is that most used. It is a very versatile oxide, particularly at low temperatures. It is volatile and great care must be taken when using earthenware glazes containing tin to check that chromium is not present—unless pink tints are acceptable!

High lead, low alumina glazes with tin oxide and chromium oxide give red or orange when low fired, 750°–800°C, a lead and soda base can give yellow. At normal earthenware temperatures and at stoneware temperatures, various dull greens are produced—they tend to

be heavy and flat and always opaque. Chrome is frequently used in prepared underglaze colours and can be useful when colouring slips.

Cobalt Oxide Co_3O_4
Cobalt Carbonate $Co\ CO_3$

Cobalt oxide, both the black and grey and cobalt carbonate give stable blues at all firing temperatures. The black cobalt oxide is the one most used. It is a very powerful flux. This, combined with the strength of colour obtained, results in only very small quantities being required. In stoneware glazes between 0.1% and 1.0% is usually sufficient, the quantity increasing with a decrease in firing temperature until up to 10% is used in some low-fired earthenware glazes.

The range of blue tints obtained varies with the glaze applied, but it tends to be hard and not altogether pleasant. The blues used on Chinese Sung and early Ming pots were soft and pleasant, due to the cobalt being impure, containing other oxides such as iron and manganese. It is often better to modify cobalt with iron and manganese. Talc is also useful although it tends to cause purple tints.

When used as an underglaze pigment it is best painted on unfired clay so that it sinks into and partly combines with the clay. When painting on biscuit it is best fixed by mixing it with Cornish stone, or a frit, or a little clay. It is a useful oxide for painting on Majolica, the tin glaze preventing any tendency of the cobalt to run.

Copper Oxide $CuO\ or\ Cu_2O$
Copper Carbonate $Cu\ CO_3$

The cupric and cuprous oxides and the carbonate are used to give a range of colours varying from greens to red. They have a slight fluxing effect and are volatile at stoneware temperatures, particularly in reduction firings; 'pink bloom' on otherwise copper-free pots can result from the presence of copper in a kiln.

Lead glazes produce a warm leaf-green when up to 4% of copper oxide is added and then fired in an oxidising firing.

Alkaline glazes produce a green/turquoise when 2–3% of copper oxide is added and fired in an oxidising firing.

DECORATION

A soda glaze, low in or free from alumina, produces a bright turquoise—like those associated with Egyptian and Persian wares. This is one of the earliest uses of copper in a glaze (3000 B.C.). The firing should be oxidising.

A lead/soda/tin glaze with 1–5% of copper oxide gives a red/purple glaze when fired in reduction at earthenware temperatures.

A clear, soft stoneware glaze with 1% of copper oxide will give a red in reduction, the red will vary from brilliant to unpleasant red/browns, much depending on the firing and base glaze used.

A high Barium glaze with copper can give some pleasant blue/greens in the stoneware range in an oxidising atmosphere. Over 5% of copper oxide gives a black metallic effect, often unpleasant.

Pigments can be made by mixing with china clay and/or talc.

Note: The addition of copper to a glaze or by painting under or over the glaze, can make soft insoluble earthenware glaze soluble and unsafe. Great care must be used, therefore, and copper is best put out of the reach of eager students, who do not understand the use of oxides and tend to be overgenerous with its application.

Iron Oxide

Red Iron	Fe_2O_3
Black Iron	Fe_3O_4
Iron Chromate	$FeCrO_4$
Yellow Ochre	$Fe_2O_3H_2O$
Crocus Martis	Fe_2O_3
Sprangles	Fe_3O_4
Yellow iron	Fe_2O_3

As can be seen, iron oxide comes in many different forms. Most are readily available from potters' merchants but most potters use only one or two types. Iron is probably the most important of the colouring oxides for it will produce a great variety of colours by mixing it with different glazes and by firing at various temperatures in oxidising or reducing atmospheres. It is also useful for modifying the tints of other pigments, such as copper and cobalt. Iron is also responsible for the colour of clays, few clays being iron free. Iron has a fluxing effect on clays and it fluxes glazes when fired in reducing atmosphere but not in an oxidising atmosphere. It is not volatile.

The most commonly used iron is red iron oxide which has a small particle size and gives an even colour. In lead glazes it gives an amber yellow to warm brown; similar, but not so bright colours are obtained with a leadless earthenware glaze. Up to 5% of iron is added.

In stoneware glazes, yellows can be obtained with the addition of up to 2% of red iron oxide, when fired in an oxidising firing. The same glaze will produce the grey/blues and greens associated with the Chinese Celadons, when fired in a reducing atmosphere; a high whiting glaze will promote blue celadon as opposed to green.

Brown, rust-reds and black are produced in a stoneware glaze by adding up to 10% of iron oxide. Reduction firing tends to promote rust-reds and oxidation promotes black but black Tenmuku glazes, which break to red on the edges of pots are usually fired in a reducing atmosphere. Black Tenmuku glaze should be high in silica, as should the clay body. It should be applied thickly. A mirror black can be obtained by the addition of 8% iron and 2% cobalt. Iron can be added to glazes by adding iron-bearing clay, such as red earthenware. Black iron behaves in a similar way to red iron.

Crocus Martis is a natural ferric oxide with larger particles which can cause a speckle in the glaze.

Iron spangles are practically insoluble and are used to produce speckle and metallic 'bursts'.

Iron chromate produces grey when used alone but is more useful for modifying other glaze pigments, such as cobalt and copper.

Yellow iron is a natural hydrated iron oxide containing some impurities and clay. It produces brown/yellows.

Manganese Dioxide MnO_2
Manganese Carbonate $MnCo_3$

The carbonate is finer grained than the dioxide so giving a smooth colour without speckle. The dioxide gives some speckle and is used more frequently than the carbonate; both give the same colour and have similar properties. Manganese is a flux up to 1,070°C when it undergoes a chemical change and ceases to be a flux; at 1,070°C it can cause bubbling on the surface of the glaze. It is volatile at high temperatures particularly in reduction, when it leaves a grey/brown colour.

A lead glaze with 2–3% of manganese dioxide gives a purple/brown colour; an alkaline glaze with 2–3% will give a purple/plum colour.

Stoneware glazes will accept up to 10% of dioxide, at which stage it gives a lustrous metallic black; smaller quantities in reduction will give grey tints. It is useful as a modifier with cobalt and copper.

Used on Majolica tin glazes as an overglaze pigment, it gives pleasant purple/browns. It is useful for colouring slips; additions of manganese, cobalt and iron being used to obtain a black slip.

Nickel Oxide NiO_2

Nickel is stable and refractory, causing mattness in a glaze. In oxidation it gives muted browns, greys and greens that are not very attractive, 1–3% of oxide being used. It is at its least attractive in a borax glaze. In reduction it is decidedly unreliable giving anything from yellow to purple, even blue. This renders it unsuitable for use except when used to modify other oxides such as cobalt, which it quietens from a hard blue to a soft grey/blue; about 0–5% should be used for this purpose.

It can be useful when used alone as an overglaze pigment on a tin glaze when it gives a green colour.

Vanadium Pentoxide V_2O_5

This pigment is not often used; when it is, it is usually combined with tin or titanium to give yellows. Depending on the yellow required amounts of 5–10% are used. The glazes tend to be opaque because of the tin or titanium present. In stoneware glazes heavy reduction can turn the oxide grey.

In a lead glaze zircon and vanadium can combine to give a blue.

Opacifiers

Opaque and matt glazes should not be confused. Matt glazes can be produced by underfiring a clear shiny glaze by adding materials such as calcium and alumina which will cause the glaze to become crystalline, small crystals form in the glaze so causing a matt surface and a resulting opacity. Such crystalline glazes are more common in stoneware but Rutile (TiO_2) will crystallise in a lead glaze when fired up to 1,050°C and is used to produce matt wall tiles.

Opaque glazes, however, result from the suspension of small particles in a glaze. These particles reflect the light and do not appreciably affect the surface of the glaze which can be shiny and not matt. The principal opacifiers are: tin, zirconium, titanium and zinc.

Tin Oxide SnO_2

Tin is the most useful opacifier both at earthenware and stoneware temperatures. It is probably best known for its use in soft earthenware Majolica glaze; it provides a milk-white background upon which pigments can be painted.

Tin increases the viscosity of a glaze, which helps prevent the running of colours. It has a tendency to crawl—if the glaze crazes as it dries crawling is likely. This tendency can be lessened by making the pot slightly damp but is best cured by reducing the shrinkage rate of the glaze. This can be done by replacing or reducing the plastic material in the glaze, normally clay. The plastic clay can be replaced with calcined clay. Some Majolica glazes have no clay content in order to avoid the risks of crawling. Opaque coloured glazes can be prepared with tin oxide.

In heavily reduced stoneware glazes tin ceases to opacify but an uneven reduction can cause patches of white.

Earthenware glazes require 5–10% of tin oxide to become opaque and stoneware glazes need 3–5%.

Chromium oxide should not be present in a kiln with white Tin glazes as the chrome and tin combine to give pinks.

Zirconium Oxide ZrO_2

Zirconium is not such a useful opacifier as tin as it gives a harsher texture and does not always favour colours as does tin. Very thorough mixing is necessary if white specks are to be avoided. Rather more zirconium is required to give the same degree of opacity, 7–12% being required.

It is best used in a glaze which is low in Boric Oxide. Like tin, it increases the tendency of a glaze to crawl so take this into account when using.

The advantages of zirconium are that it is much cheaper than tin and it avoids the danger of chrome/tin pinks. It is used in the manufacture of kiln furniture and can be used as a batt wash by using 10 parts zircon to one part china clay.

Titanium Oxide TiO_2

Titanium is not frequently used in glazes but is very useful if a matt surface as well as an opaque glaze is required. It gives a creamy/buff colour in earthenware when 8–9% is added, it dulls colouring oxides, making copper a dull brown.

Rutile (titanium containing some iron), gives a darker colour. In stoneware, titanium (5%) can produce creamy whites with a vellum surface. In an oxidising firing rutile gives some warmth that is lacking if titanium is used.

In stoneware, titanium can react with an iron glaze, such as celadon or Tenmuku, to give blue 'Chün' effects, sometimes pleasant, sometimes very sickly.

Zinc Oxide ZnO

Zinc is a useful flux when used in quantities of up to 2%. It affects the colouring pigments, making iron muddy and dull but causing copper and cobalt to give an interesting range of colours. It is used in lead free 'Bristol' glazes as flux and opacifier.

Zinc can be used in larger quantities in earthenware and stoneware to give matt opaque glazes. Great care must be taken to avoid blistering and crawling. Probably better used in combination with tin and titanium.

Plate 37. Coiled Peruvian earthenware jar, with brown painted slip on white ground.

SETTING-UP A SCHOOL POTTERY

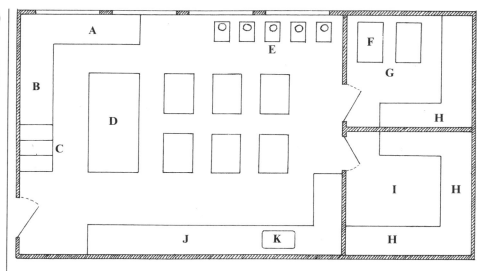

Fig. 42. Suggested layout for a school pottery. Ideal layouts are seldom possible but ample storage and shelving is essential.

A Bench
B Pug-mill
C Clay bins
D Wedging and kneading bench
E Wheels
F Kiln
G Kiln Room
H Shelving
I Damp room and clay store
J Bench for glazing. Shelves over, cupboards under.
K Sink

If pottery, or indeed any other craft, is to be taught in school it is essential that two prerequisites are satisfied.

1. Time

Sufficient time must be available to the teacher and students, either in or out of school hours, so that the craft can be undertaken with some degree of continuity and application. It is quite hopeless to have groups of students for only 30–45 minutes, for they no sooner get involved in their work than they are having to clear up. An hour is the shortest useful time but for secondary and high school pupils half a day is to be preferred.

Closely connected with prerequisite number 2 is that the number of students using the pottery room should not exceed the number of useful working areas. Pottery-making requires a minimum of about a square metre (1 square yard) per student although small primary school pupils could probably manage with less. If the pottery room is of normal classroom size 15–20 students will fill it to over-flowing! It is sometimes difficult persuading headmasters that 30–40 students cannot be accommodated for pottery at one time but if they are invited to see a class in action, particularly when the clay is being wedged and kneaded, they frequently sympathise with the pottery teacher's argument and make arrangements that will reduce the size of the class to a manageable number.

2. Basic equipment

It is essential that the necessary basic equipment is available before pottery is undertaken. It seems quite pointless to include pottery in a school curriculum if the pot cannot be fired either in a professionally manufactured kiln or in a home-made outdoor kiln. As has been stressed elsewhere, pottery incorporates clay preparation, making of pots and forms, biscuit-firing, glazing and glaze-firing.

The basic equipment and facilities for setting up a school pottery are:
a) A room of adequate size, preferably on the ground floor. Kilns and clay are heavy, so a lot of heavy carrying and wasted time will be saved if the room is both on the ground floor and near to a delivery entrance.

The room should be almost exclusively

used for pottery and clay sculpture, for clay is messy and whilst a pottery should be well organised and tidy it is extremely difficult to use the room for clean work such as drawing.

The floor should be non-dust harbouring and suitable for washing down. Health and safety inspectors are naturally concerned about the dangers of silicosis which can result from inhaling fine particles of silica over a long period of time. Such particles are present in clay dust and some glaze ingredients, notably quartz and flint. It is therefore essential that the floor can be washed daily, so keeping the dust to a minimum.

If a pottery-room is to be built or a room properly adapted, the floor should be of quarry tiles or smooth concrete with a floor gully into which the water used for swilling down the floor can be swept.

b) A small room for use as a kiln room. A separate room for kilns is essential if a gas kiln is to be used and desirable if electric kilns are to be used. The fumes from kilns can be unpleasant if breathed for long periods but if an electric kiln can only be installed in the pottery studio and nowhere else, it is worth tolerating the fumes for the sake of having the use of the kiln. If a storeroom is used as a kiln room ensure that there is sufficient ventilation either from windows or an extractor fan.

c) A storeroom or storage area for clay and glaze materials. If a storeroom near to the pottery-room can be used this is ideal; if such a room is not available perhaps a storeroom elsewhere or under the school hall can be utilised. Wherever the store is it must be cool so as to ensure that the clay is not dried out. If the store-room is cool and the clay is kept wrapped in plastic bags, it will be suitable for use for a year and more.

d) A kiln. Assuming that prerequisites a to c are available, a kiln is the single most essential piece of equipment for all potters. The type of kiln bought will depend on the money available, the number of possible students and hence the volume of work likely to require firing. If 100 secondary school students use the pottery studio for about $1\frac{1}{2}$ hours each per week, a kiln or kilns having a total capacity of .17m^3 (6 cu ft) is about the minimum capacity with which to keep reasonably up-to-date with firing, assum-ing that the kiln or kilns are fired on average twice a week, sometimes three times in one week. Remember that most work requires both a biscuit- and glaze-firing, and that glaze packing takes up more kiln space than a biscuit-firing, since the pots must not touch each other.

e) Work benches. Heavy, sturdy benches are to be preferred. The easiest type to keep clean are those covered with formica but many potters like to work on a slate or marble slab. Such slabs can sometimes be bought, or even obtained free, when older property is being demolished.

If formica topped benches are used, it is essential to have one bench with a slate, concrete or hardwood top upon which to knead. Formica or any other sealed surface is unsuitable for kneading as the clay will stick to the bench. Ideally the kneading bench should be rather lower than the working benches, about 60 cm (24 in) from the ground. This permits the whole weight of the body to be used when kneading, and not just pressure from the arms.

As far as possible a bench area of 1 square metre (1 square yard) should be allowed for each student, plus a bench for wedging and kneading.

f) Shelving. Adequate storage shelves or cupboards are essential. When the pots or forms have been made, they must be left to dry out on a shelf where they will not be damaged. When the work has been biscuit-fired it must be stored until the students attend the class to apply glazes. The work must then be stored until it can be glaze-fired. Finally, the finished work has to be stored until it is taken away by the students.

A cupboard for storing unfinished work is also very desirable, if not essential. If most work is hand-built an ordinary cupboard is satisfactory as the work can be wrapped in plastic sheeting to keep it damp. However, if the pots are thrown on the wheel they are far too delicate and soft to be wrapped in plastic, so a damp-cupboard is necessary. Such a cupboard has to keep damp inside it, and be so constructed that warm dry air is kept out. These conditions can be achieved by lining a cupboard with strong plastic sheeting; making plaster-of-Paris shelves which can be regularly soaked with water, and by ensuring that the doors fit well and are kept closed.

g) Storage bins. Storage bins are required for clay, glazes and dry materials. The size and type of bin depends on the amount of pottery to be undertaken. Plastic dustbins or trash cans are suitable for glaze and dry material storage. It is far easier to glaze when the pots can be dipped into a deep bin of glaze, so even when only small groups are able to pot, generous bins of glaze are best prepared.

Clay needs to be stored in an airtight bin, and clay for reclaiming needs to be soaked in a strong water-tight bin. Plastic bins are suitable for storing prepared clay but such bins are rarely suitable for soaking down clay for reclamation as the weight of clay and water and the use of a trowel or spade to dig out the wet clay soon splits the bin. A cold water tank, fibre glass or galvanised iron, makes an ideal reclamation bin. If the pottery-room is fully used it will be necessary to have two tanks, as it is better to leave a tank of wet, freshly soaked clay to mature and dry out a little before spreading out the clay on absorbent boards to firm-up for pugging or kneading. The tanks can be mounted on wheels so that they can be moved.

h) Boards. Boards of various sizes and materials are essential in any pottery

Plate 38. Children generally find pottery classes both interesting and fun. Many show pleasing aptitude for the basic skills.

SETTING-UP A SCHOOL POTTERY

room. Absorbent boards upon which wet clay can be dried prior to pugging or kneading and which can be used as kneading boards for clay that is just slightly too damp for use, are a must. Absorbent asbestos board is ideal for this purpose. The smooth finished type 2 cm ($\frac{3}{4}$ in) thick can be bought as a large sheet and cut into pieces. Care must be taken to wear a simple mask as the asbestos dust can be a health hazard. Once in use the asbestos is slightly damp and is not cut or scored so there is little, if any health hazard.

Boards upon which to build coil and slab pots are also necessary. These can be round or square, of various sizes, and of any material that will not warp or break up when made wet. Marine ply-wood or hard asbestos are probably the best materials to use, but any plywood off-cuts will suffice. Round batts are usually expensive so they are an extravagance except for use on the potters' wheel.

Boards upon which to place thrown pots are also necessary if a potters' wheel is available.

i) Equipment for making slices of clay. Hessian or pieces of old sheets are needed to prevent clay from sticking to the bench as it is made into slices. Rolling-pins or cardboard tubing and strips of wood to act as thickness guides and thin wire or nylon fishing wire with a toggle at each end are needed for preparing slices of clay.

j) Bench whirlers or banding wheels. These are not essential pieces of equipment but they are very useful when making coil pots, or decorating a pot. Traditionally the potter walked around a coil pot as it was made but the space in a pottery-room does not normally permit this. Being able to turn the pot around on a whirler is a suitable substitute method requiring far less space. Whirlers or banding-wheels are very useful when decorating, particularly when painting continuous bands around a pot. Many potters also use banding-wheels when applying wax resist, prior to glazing.

The difference between a whirler and a banding-wheel is that the whirler is placed on a bench whereas the banding-wheel is on an adjustable stand.

k) Potters' wheels. It certainly is not essential to have potters' wheels in order to make pots—this is made clear in Chapter 4. Primary schools have no need of a wheel for young children are invariably too small to use a wheel, and they are usually much better at inventing forms than thinking out suitable functional forms to make on the wheel. Secondary and high schools that undertake very little pottery would also be wasting money if they indulged in a wheel. The money would almost certainly be better spent on a larger or additional kiln.

Those schools that have one or more instructors teaching pottery full-time may find wheels beneficial if the students are able to spend an adequate amount of time gaining the basic skills of throwing. There are many types of wheel available, from a large number of manufacturers. The two main types are power-driven and kick-wheels. Both types are available with or without a seat for the potter. Whilst personal preference and experience plays a large part in deciding which wheel to buy, I am sure most potters would agree that a kick-wheel without a seat is really not very useful. Standing on one foot and kicking with the other foot is no easy task, and can be very tiring. The 'Leach' type kick-wheel is well-tried and popular among those who do not use a power-driven wheel, but it requires an operator with fairly long legs to operate it comfortably, so it is only suitable for the older, secondary school student.

There are many electrically-driven wheels on the market, ranging from the large heavy cone-driven wheels that are or were used in industry, to light-weight table models. Cone-driven wheels are excellent but usually far too expensive for school use and light-weight table models are not recommended for schools. About midway in the price range is the wheel driven by a D.C. motor with the speed controlled electronically as opposed to mechanically. Such wheels are now available from a number of suppliers, each offering different refinements, finishes and degrees of comfort. This type of wheel requires little maintenance, always an advantage.

l) A pug-mill. A pug-mill becomes a necessity if pottery is to be undertaken on a large scale. If an instructor is teaching pottery or any sort of clay work full-time, the amount of clay requiring reclamation will be such that a pug-mill is essential unless a lot of time is to be spent wedging and kneading clay ready for use.

Most potters' suppliers market pug-mills but the main choice is between a horizontal and a vertical type, the barrel of the former being horizontal and requiring a plate and lever to push the clay into the barrel. The barrel of the vertical type, being vertical, does not require a plate and lever to feed in the clay as gravity assists the downward direction of the clay. Vertical pug-mills are therefore easier and quicker to use but they are considerably more expensive. If the cost of the teacher's or technical assistants' time is taken into account, they are probably cheaper.

The size of the barrel and nozzle of both types varies—the larger the nozzle the greater the output of clay per hour. The size chosen will depend on the amount of clay that is likely to require pugging and the money available but it always seems advisable to get a pug-mill with an output greater than is thought necessary, for it is amazing how the amount of clay requiring reclaiming builds up and pugging is a boring necessity. Hand-operated pug-mills are available; such models are turned by hand instead of by an electric motor. It is easier to wedge and knead the clay than to use such a machine.

m) Sundry items. All sorts of odds and ends are useful to the potter. Some of the more obvious items are sponges and bowls for cleaning up and for use when throwing on the wheel; thin stainless steel wire cut into 30 cm (1 ft) lengths with a wooden toggle at each end for cutting the clay; wooden modelling tools; pieces of hack-saw blade for scraping pots and for decorating; and innumerable objects which will make decorative impressions when pressed into soft clay.

The preceding headings give the basic requirements of accommodation and equipment for a school pottery. In addition basic services such as water, suitable drainage and electrical services, possibly including three phase supply, need to be available. If the room, benches, kiln, clay storage and clay are available pottery can start.

THE POTTER'S HERITAGE

The history and development of pottery is closely linked with the general development of man and his cultures. In the chapters dealing with the making and decorating of pots, particular techniques and forms are frequently referred to, but a more general assessment of the craft as it has developed over the centuries, can provide a valuable background to a better understanding of its possibilities.

What follows is a brief summary and all students of pottery are urged to read more specialised books on the history and development of ceramics and always to associate such developments with the general development of a culture, and the interplay of one culture with another.

CHINESE POTTERY

Both technically and aesthetically, Far Eastern pottery is unsurpassed. Chinese pottery in particular has been and continues to be a great source of inspiration.

The principal Chinese Dynasties

HAN	*206B.C. –A.D.220*
Disturbed period	*A.D.220 –A.D.618*
T'ANG	*A.D.618 –A.D.906*
SUNG	*A.D.907 –A.D.1279*
YUAN (Mongol)	*A.D.1280–A.D.1368*
MING	*A.D.1368–A.D.1644*
CHING (Manchu)	*A.D.1644–A.D.1912*

Chinese pottery is invariably named after the dynastic period during which it was made, sometimes more specifically after a Emperor or a dynasty. When it is noted that wares that have been regarded as classical were being made in *Han* times, the vastness of the subject is realised.

HAN period

Large granary wares and wine jars made in the style of earlier bronzes. Some wares lead glazed and stained with copper.

Porcelain was probably discovered in this period. Kilns built through hillsides, refinement of materials and the patronage of the Imperial court led to the vitrification, resonance and translucency we in the West associate with porcelain.

CHAPTER 13

Plate 39. Pot of Chinese Han dynasty (206 B.C. to A.D. 220).

T'ANG period

An outburst of creative activity in this period following the wars of the disturbed period. Standard of Chinese ceramics set. Increased contact with the West, for T'ang wares have been found in Egypt. Lead glazed wares were mostly mottled green/brown on a white body. Clays of different colour were mixed to make 'marbled' or 'Agate' ware. Porcelain was creamy white with celadon and amber glazes. Moulded relief was used. The body was sometimes engraved then filled with glaze. Glaze often ended in a wavy line short of the base.

Hellenistic influence on some wares, e.g. amphora-shaped vases.

Most examples of T'ang ware were not excavated until the construction of the railways, when many tombs were disturbed. However, the Emperors of Ming and Ching dynasties built up collections of earlier work.

SUNG period

This was a period of great achievement in philosophy and the arts, but rather backward-looking and withdrawn, which resulted in pottery being reminiscent of early jade and bronzes. They sought to make pottery with the hardness, durability, resonance, dim translucency and even the colours of jade. From this resulted the famous Sung

THE POTTER'S HERITAGE

celadon wares. Stoneware pots of great beauty were also made, with a black/brown glaze (Tenmuku). Free, swift brushwork was used for decoration.

Sung ware is claimed to be the best pottery ever made, both by Western collections and Japanese Tea-masters. The following are some of the more famous Sung wares: Ju, Kuan, Ko, Lungchuan, Chün (blue), Chien, Ting (white).

YUAN dynasty *(Mongols)*
Sung ware remained in fashion but they supplied a wider market, for much of Asia was under Mongol rule. Persian influence on decoration, in particular the use of cobalt for painting on porcelain.

MING dynasty
To begin with during this period, the Chinese were forward-looking and creative. They rejected Sung taste in favour of T'ang and brighter colours. In some ways the Ming period was to T'ang as our Renaissance was to classical Greece and Rome. The Imperial Court ordered fine white porcelain decorated with cobalt (blue) and coloured enamels. Pots and glazes of the T'ang period were copied which often makes the dating very difficult. Pots were exported, the foreign market often dictating the shape and decoration. The greatest collections of Ming 'Blue and White' were made by the Sultans of Turkey and Egypt, and are now in Istanbul. After the

Japanese invasion of China (1592–98) the Ming period became backward looking.

CHING dynasty *(Manchu rulers)*
Under the Emperor K'ang Hsi came a great flourishing of all the arts, including pottery. Processes were the same as in the Ming period. A few new glazes were used and slight variation in shapes. The early porcelains had fine flowing lines, were superbly made and the decoration was as bold and fresh as the best Ming porcelain.

As time went on large grotesque forms with finicky decoration were made in response to European demands. Over-refinement and 'cleverness' became all-important (Chien Lung), which although perfect marvels of manipulative skill did not result in pleasing pottery.

Chinese influence
Chinese artistic influence was paramount over most of S.E. Asia, Korea and Japan. However the Japanese developed their own pottery wares, which were usually much simpler than those of China.

PRE-HISTORIC WARE
Pottery, as we know it, played no part in the lives of the wandering hunters and food-collectors who lived during the old and middle Stone Ages.

The first consistent use of pottery came with the discovery of agriculture and the domestication of animals, which enabled men to live in settled communities, say from about 8000 B.C.

Most examples of Neolithic and Early Iron Age pottery have been found in domestic sites, whereas Bronze Age pottery is usually found in burial sites (Long Barrows).

The Potters' Wheel did not come to Britain until the late Early Iron Age, consequently most pottery was hand-built, probably by women. The wares were round-based, unglazed, sometimes with burnished slip. Decoration was often geometric in inspiration and either incised or impressed.

EGYPTIAN WARES
The earliest pottery—Tasian Ware—derived from basketry, as did pre-historic pottery. Clay was daubed and pressed onto baskets, then crudely

fired. Basket-like forms persist to the present day.

During the later Badarian culture, notable black-topped wares were produced. These outstanding pots appear to be derived from stone forms and the black top was caused by the flames causing reduction to the inverted rim during the firing process. (Reduction = lack of oxygen.) Slip was used a little later as was the first glaze.

GREEK WARES
Greek pottery is famous for its figured decoration executed in glossy black on fired clay; this dark slip was almost a glaze, being a very fine clay containing iron and potash (from wood ash). The pots were fired to earthenware

Plate 41. Greek Attic-ware amphora of Late Geometric period, 720–700 B.C.

Plate 40. Porcelain stem cup of Chinese Ming dynasty (early 14th century).

Plate 42. Greek Attic-ware dating from the beginning of 5th century B.C.

temperatures in an oxidising atmosphere —reduction atmosphere—re-oxidising atmosphere. However, a majority of Greek pottery was simple in form and decoration, having simple incised bands and no figures.

The shapes reflect the function. For example, the *Hydria* was a water jar with two handles for lifting the pot onto the head and carrying, and a third handle was for pouring. *Krater* was a bowl for mixing wine and water. *Amphora* was for oil storage etc. and had a narrow neck to prevent excessive evaporation.

The potters' wheel was used for most Greek pottery, a very high standard being achieved.

Despite the satisfactory balance and proportion of Greek vases, they lack a feeling for the use of plastic clay. This may be due to the inspiration obtained from the silver and gold wares that were so highly prized.

ROMAN WARES

As in so many things, the Romans imitated the Greeks in their pottery forms and decoration. However, their *Samian* wares are notable. These wares were relief-moulded, smooth, gloss-red earthenware which was originated by the *Etruscans*. It was ultimately made

all over the Roman Empire, including Britain. The red gloss was obtained by dipping the raw pot into a suspension of siliceous clay which fused when fired, so forming a simple glaze.

Domestic ware of this period, including water jars and lamps have survived in considerable quantities, as have Roman bricks, tiles and hypocaust.

EUROPEAN POTTERY

After the collapse of the Roman Empire there was no major development in European pottery until the Moorish invasion of Spain.

The Moors were Arabs from North Africa, who were greatly influenced by Islamic work, being Moslems themselves. They are best-known for the magnificent buildings they constructed in Spain, e.g. the Alhambra in Granada.

Spanish lustre ware reached Italy via Majorca, hence the name *Majolica* ware. (Any ware with overglaze painting on a tin glaze is called *Majolica*.) Another name for a similar ware is *Faience*, from the name 'Faenza' where green Florentine ware was made.

Dutch *Delftware* is a later Majolica and is an imitation of Chinese Ming Blue and White ware. Such ware was also manufactured in Bristol and Liverpool, England.

Salt glaze ware was first made on a

Plate 43. Roman Samian-ware made in Somme, France in 2nd century A.D. It has incised floral decoration in imitation of cut glass.

Plate 44. English salt-glaze bottle made by Dwight in Fulham about A.D. 1670.

large scale in Cologne. Common salt was thrown into the kiln when it reached its maximum temperature; the salt combined with the silica in the clay to form a glaze.

Slip-ware, although used in Medieval times, reached its culmination in Staffordshire in Britain during the 18th century. Of red body, it has bold vigorous pattern trailed on it with white and other coloured clays, rather like icing on a cake. The best pieces were by the Toft and Simpson families.

Staffordshire earthenware underwent tremendous refinement in the 18th and 19th centuries. Josiah Wedgwood's *Cream Ware* (called 'Queens' under the patronage of Queen Charlotte) which was cheap, durable and functional, stole all markets and set the highest standards for present-day industrial ware.

Cream ware was earthenware with a lead glaze using a white clay body, the same as used for salt-glaze stoneware, that is ball clay and calcined flint. Such clay was developed at the Fulham Pottery in the 17th century by John Dwight for making salt-glaze stoneware

THE POTTER'S HERITAGE

in an attempt to rival imported German salt-glaze ware and the red stoneware teapots imported from China. Fulham made use of moulded decoration which was to be used so much by Wedgwood. Wedgwood used a high biscuit-firing

Plate 45. English medieval jug found in Oxford.

Plate 46. Large storage pot from the palace at Knossos in Crete. It is 5ft (180cm) high.

and low glaze-firing, so reducing kiln losses and enabling him to apply the glaze very thinly.

Cream ware was later used by Thomas Whieldon, the greatest potting genius of his age. He is better known as the teacher of Joseph Spode and Josiah Wedgwood. Wedgwood later became Whieldon's partner (1754–59). When Wedgwood set up by himself he concentrated on glazing other people's ware. He improved cream ware which he glazed then sent to Liverpool for transfer decoration. He later had cream ware enamelled and gilded.

In the 1760's the architects Robert and John Adam introduced classical themes of decoration and building styles. Wedgwood quickly adapted his work to this style.

He introduced his 'basaltes', i.e. pots classical in form and decoration which were underglazed black and were stoneware. Some were known as Etruscan ware due to the decoration used. Jasper Ware was also developed. This was white stoneware which could be coloured right through with metal oxide. Later only a surface wash of the coloured clay was applied to the white pot. Pale blue, dark blue, sage green, lilac, yellow and black wares were made. Onto these colours white decoration was applied, often in the form of Greek figures and leaves. This is the ware we still see produced by Wedgwood.

The potters' wheel continued to be used but some wares were slip-moulded. That is, plaster-of-Paris moulds were made from fired and glazed master moulds. Slip was poured onto the mould and allowed to form a coating of the required thickness on the plaster. This is the method often used in mass production today.

EUROPEAN PORCELAIN

Due to the import of Chinese porcelain, which was expensive, many Europeans sought to make porcelain. This proved impossible at first but a soft paste porcelain was eventually made under the patronage of the Medicis in Florence. Soft paste can be scored with a steel point. This ware was later made in France and Germany. Eventually Böttger, working in Saxony, discovered kaolin and so established the Meissen

factory which produced 'hard-paste' porcelain.

The earliest English examples were produced in 1745 at Chelsea. These were metallic in form, the makers and backers being former goldsmiths.

ENGLISH PORCELAIN

Chelsea

The first English porcelain was made in Chelsea. Whereas the European factories were promoted by royal patrons, Chelsea was started by a group of business men and goldsmiths. This accounts for the metal forms of some of the Chelsea wares. The work was usually highly decorated, enamelling and gilding being used. By the 1750's decorative figures were being made, often inspired by Meissen products.

The factory mark of 'Chelsea' was an anchor.

Bow and Bone China

In 1749 a patent was taken out by the Bow factory which mentioned a material produced partly by 'calcining all animal substance'. In other words, the first use of bone ash, which produced Bone China, Englands greatest contribution in the field of porcelain manufacture.

The advantages of Bone China are that it can be high-fired in the biscuit-firing, whilst all the pots are packed in sand to prevent warping and cracking. It can then be low-fired in the glaze-firing, thus the high wastage rate of traditional porcelain, which is caused by the high glaze-firing, is reduced and porcelain becomes a cheaper commodity within the purchasing power of an increased market.

Bristol and Worcester

The Bristol and Worcester factories combined in 1752. The porcelain body included soap rock from Cornwall, which gave the ware a green colour by transmitted light.

This factory was the first to use enamel transfers on a large scale.

Derby

This factory was established in 1750 to produce transfer decorated ware, often copies of Meissen, and copies of the white unglazed Sevres figures.

Spode

This factory developed in Stoke on Trent, the Bone China introduced by the Chelsea Factory.

APPENDIX ONE

USEFUL INFORMATION

Pyrometric Cones

These cones are made of ceramic material and are Time/Temperature indicators. They do not, like a pyrometer, measure the temperature in the kiln at a given moment in time but measure effects of heat when applied for varying periods of time. The chemical changes that occur in clay and glazes vary with the rate at which the temperature is increased as well as the actual temperature, so cones give a far better indication of when glazes are likely to be mature than a pyrometer.

A wide range of cones is available with squatting temperatures of 600°C to 1,500°C, the steps between cones varying from 10°C to 50°C. All cones are numbered so that the correct cones can be identified.

Three cones of consecutive numbers should be used, the second cone indicating the finishing point of the firing. They are placed either in stands supplied by potters' merchants or in a piece of grogged clay. They should lean at an angle of 10° and be placed where they can be seen through the kiln spy-hole. When the second cone has bent over so that its tip is touching the stand the firing is complete. The first cone acts as a warning that the firing is near completion and the third cone indicates how much, if any, the kiln has been over-fired.

The principal cones available are the English Harrisons' Staffordshire cones, and the American Orton cones. The cone reference numbers and approximate squatting temperatures are indicated on the right for the cones more commonly used:

Staff cone	Temperature °C	Orton cone
220	600	020
210	650	019
200	670	
190	690	018
180	710	
170	730	017
160	750	016
165	760	
150	790	015
155	800	
140	815	014
130	835	013
120	855	012
110	880	011
100	900	009
090	920	008
080	940	
085	950	
070	960	007
075	970	
060	980	006
065	990	
050	1,000	
055	1,010	
040	1,020	005
045	1,030	
030	1,040	004
035	1,050	
020	1,060	003
025	1,070	
010	1,080	
10	1,100	002
15	1,110	001
20	1,120	101
25	1,130	102
30	1,140	103
35	1,150	
40	1,160	104
45	1,170	105
50	1,180	
55	1,190	
60	1,200	106
65	1,215	107
70	1,230	108
75	1,240	
80	1,250	109
85	1,260	
87	1,270	
90	1,280	110
95	1,290	
100	1,300	111

NOTE: The rate at which the temperature rises affects Staffordshire and Orton cones in slightly different ways, so the equivalents for the two types of cone are only approximate.

APPENDIX TWO

BOOK LIST FOR FURTHER READING

A Potter's Book	Bernard Leach	Faber & Faber
Pioneer Pottery	Michael Cardew	Longmans
An Illustrated Dictionary of Practical Pottery	Robert Fournier	Van Nostrand Reinhold
Technique of Throwing	John Colbeck	Batsford
Pottery in Britain Today	Michael Casson	Tiranti
Art and Technique of Raku	H. Reigger	Studio Vista
Artist Potters in England	M. Rose	Faber & Faber
A History of Pottery	E. Cooper	Longmans
Technique of Pottery	D. Billington	
A Handbook of Pottery	E. Cooper	Longmans
Clay and Glazes for the Potter	Daniel Rhodes	Pitman
Stoneware and Porcelain	Daniel Rhodes	Pitman
Kilns: Design, Construction and Operation	Daniel Rhodes	Pitman
The Art of the Modern Potter	Tony Birks	Country Life
Kenzan and his Tradition	Bernard Leach	Faber & Faber
The World of Japanese Ceramics	Herbert Saunders	Ward Lock
Ceramics—A Potter's Handbook	G. Nelson	Holt Rinehart and Winston
Spanish Folk Ceramics	Jose Lorens Antiga and Jose Corredor-Mathias	Editorial Bhume Barcelona
The Unknown Craftsman	B. Leach/S. Yanagi	Kodansha International Ltd.
Tin Glaze Pottery in Europe and the Islamic World	Alan Caiger-Smith	Faber & Faber
Ceramic Review	Published bi-monthly by Craftsmen Potters Association	

SOME COMMON GLAZE INGREDIENTS AND THEIR PROPERTIES

Material	Formula	Mol. Weight	Fluxing Ability	Expansion	Contains	%	Comment
Aluminium Oxide	Al_2O_3	102	Very Refractory	Low	Al_2O_3	100	1. Affects degree of fluidity of molten mass, therefore its stability. 2. Controls matting and refractoriness. 3. Acts either as base or acid in molecular formula. 4. Calcined alumina in glaze curbs crystallising and reduces tendency to crawl. A useful batt wash.
Barium Carbonate	$BaCO_3$	197	Low	Low	BaO	79	1. Produces glass with high index of refraction therefore more brilliant than other earths. 2. A matting agent in excess.
Barium Oxide	BaO	153	Low	Low	BaO	100	As for Barium Carbonate.
Bentonite	$Al_2O_3\ 4SiO_2$ $H_2O + nH_2O$			High			1. Very plastic, useful for improving plasticity of clay, particularly porcelain. 2. About 2% added to a glaze acts as a deflocculant, keeping the glaze in suspension.
Bone Ash Calcium Phosphate	$3CaO\ P_2O_5$	310	Low	Medium	CaO P_2O_5	54 46	Small bubbles induce opacity, even opalescence. Pitting and pinholing when used in excess. Used in Bone China bodies. A glass former.
Borax dehydrated	$Na_2O\ 2B_2O_3$ or $Na_2O\ B_4O_7$	202	High	Low	$2B_2O_3$ N_2O	69 31	1. Soluble, therefore of limited use but is useful for lower fusion point of a glaze. 2. Most useful when incorporated into a frit for earthenware glazes.
Boric Oxide	B_2O_3	70	High	Low or Negative	B_2O_3	100	1. Can give opalescent and broken effects. 2. Intensifies colour. 3. Can be used over a wide range of temperatures. 4. Increases the elasticity of a glaze and so lowers tendency to craze.
Calcium Oxide	CaO	56	Low	Medium	CaO	100	1. Refractory by itself. Increases hardness of glaze. 2. Rarely absent from stoneware glazes. Activity increases with other oxides on rise in temperature. 3. Increases tensile strength and lowers coefficient of thermal expansion in relation to alkalis. 4. In excess it increases refractoriness and causes mattness and then crystallisation. 5. Frequently provided in the form of Whiting ($CaCO_3$).

Material	Formula				Oxide	%	Notes
China Clay Kaolin	Varies Theoretical Al_2O_3 $2SiO_2$ $2H_2O$	258		Low	Al_2O_3 SiO_2 Al_2O_3	39.5 46.5 43.9	1. Large particle size prevent plasticity. 2. Can cause glaze to crawl if used in excess. 3. Useful in glaze to help it adhere to the biscuited pot and provides silica and alumina
Calcined	Al_2O_3 $2SiO_2$	222			SiO_2	54.1	4. Used to raise fluxing temperature in glaze.
Colemanite	$2CaO$ $3B_2O_3$ $5H_2O$	412	Strong	Low	CaO B_2O	27.5 50.7	1. Only non-soluble form of Boric Oxide. 2. A powerful flux. 3. Intensifies colour. 4. Reduces thermal expansion so reduces risk of crazing. 5. Can produce broken and streaked colour. 6. Unpredictable in large quantities, when it can cause crawling. 7. Gerstley Borate is a reliable colemanite found in U.S.A.
Cornish Stone Pegmatite	NaK_2O Al_2O_3 $8SiO_2$ (variable)	644	Good	Medium	NaK_2O Al_2O_3 SiO_2	variable	1. A felspar found in England. 2. Usually free of iron. 3. Contains fluorspar and mica, the former often giving a bluish colour to the raw material. 4. Frequently the main flux in stoneware and the secondary flux in earthenware. 5. Highly viscous so preventing the glaze from becoming too fluid.
Dolomite Carbonate of calcium and magnesium	$Ca CO_3$ $Mg CO_3$	184	Good	Low	CaO MgO	31 22	1. A naturally occurring material the analysis of which may vary. 2. An insoluble source of Magnesium and Calcium. 3. Used in stoneware glazes both as a flux and for giving the glaze a pleasing matt surface.
Felspar 1. Potash. Orthoclase	K_2O Al_2O_3 $6SiO_2$	556	Good	Medium	K_2O Al_2O_3 SiO_2	16.9 18.3 64.8	1. All the felspar are minerals with an alumina/silica base but with a varying basic flux, this can be Potash, Soda or Calcium but more than one flux is usually present.
2. Soda. Albite	Na_2O Al_2O_3 $6SiO_2$	524	Good		Na_2O Al_2O_3 SiO_2	11.8 19.4 68.8	2. With Cornish stone, the felspars provide one of the main stoneware fluxes. 3. Highly viscous so preventing the glaze from becoming too fluid.
3. Lime. Anorthite	CaO Al_2O_3 $2SiO_2$	278	Good		CaO Al_2O_3 SiO_2	20.4 36.4 22.8	
Lead Oxide Litharge	PbO	223	Very High	Low	PbO	100	1. Seldom used due to being poisonous. 2. Usually made into a lead frit which is safe when used correctly and is insoluble. 3. High brilliance due to high refractive index.

Material	Formula	Mol. Weight	Fluxing Ability	Expansion	Contains	%	Comment
							4. Very active flux.
							5. In reduction it boils and bubbles, volatilising above 1200°C.
Lithium Oxide	Li_2O	30	High	Low	Li_2O	100	1. A very strong flux, as strong as soda.
							2. Low expansion rate reduces risk of crazing.
							3. Colour behaviour similar to that of soda.
							4. Useful in earthenware and stoneware glazes for reducing the melting point.
							5. Much more expensive than soda.
Magnesium Oxide	MgO	40	Low	Very Low	MgO	100	1. Acts as a flux at high temperatures.
							2. A matting agent when in excess of .3 molecular equivalent of RO.
							3. Can give pleasant buttery surface to glaze.
							4. Usually introduced to glaze in Talc and in Dolomite.
Nepheline Syenite	$Na_2O\ Al_2O_3\ 2SiO_2$	462	Good	Medium	Na_2O Al_2O_3 SiO_2	variable	1. The formula is theoretical and some potash is invariably present.
							2. High in alumina and soda compared with most felspars.
							3. Tends to have a lower melting point than most felspars so is useful when the melting point of a glaze is to be lowered.
							4. Useful in bodies when felspar content tends to cause shivering.
Potassium Oxide	K_2O	94	High	High	K_2O	100	1. More refractory than sodium oxide. Increases hardness of glaze. Strong flux.
							2. Lower expansion than soda so more can be used.
							3. Soluble, therefore must be fritted or obtained from mineral containing potash, e.g. felspars.
							4. Present in most stoneware glazes.
Silicon dioxide (silica)	SiO_2	60	Very re-fractory	Low	SiO_2	100	1. The glass former in glazes.
							2. Forms important part of clay bodies.
							3. Present in many glaze materials but is also derived from flint and quartz.
Sodium Oxide	Na_2O	62	High	Very High	Na_2O	100	1. A strong flux present in many glazes.
							2. Very high expansion rate so tends to cause crazing.
							3. Decreases tensile strength and elasticity, producing a brittle glaze.

4. Increases refractive index, therefore the brilliance of a glaze.
5. Necessary when producing turquoise from copper oxide.
6. Soluble so must be fritted or obtained from soda bearing mineral such as the felspars.

Strontium Oxide	SrO	104	Good	Low	SrO	100	1. When replacing calcium on a molecular basis it increases fluidity and solubility. 2. Can be used as one of the bases in an earthenware glaze. 3. The non-poisonous carbonate is normally used. 4. More expensive than calcium.
Talc	$3MgO\ 4SiO_2$ H_2O	379	Good in small amounts	Low	MgO SiO_2	32 63	1. With dolomite the source of Magnesium in glazes. 2. In small quantities, 2%, it acts as a flux. 3. In larger quantities makes glaze more viscous. 4. Low thermal expansion helps prevent crazing. 5. Gives the glaze a buttery surface.
Whiting	$CaCO_3$	100	Good	Medium	$CaCO_3$	100	1. The chief source of calcium in glazes. See calcium oxide.
Zinc Oxide	ZnO	81	Good in small amounts	Low	ZnO	100	1. An active flux in small quantities, 2%. 2. Forms crystals in saturation and so mattness. 3. Used to replace lead in Bristol glazes which are used for sanitary ware, etc. 4. Raw material has high shrinkage which makes application of glaze difficult so is best calcined.

The Oxides and Carbonates commonly used in Ceramics

	Formula	Molecular weight
Aluminium Oxide	Al_2O_3	102
Antimony Oxide	SbO_3	291
Barium Oxide	BaO	153
Barium Carbonate	$Ba\ CO_3$	198
Boric Oxide	B_2O_3	70
Calcium Oxide	CaO	56
Calcium Carbonate	$CaCO_3$	100
Chromium Oxide	Cr_2O_3	152
Cobalt Oxide	Co_3O_4	241
Cobalt Carbonate	$CoCO_3$	119
Copper Oxide	CuO	80
Copper Carbonate	$CuCO_3$	124
Iron Oxide	Fe_2O_3	160
Iron Chromate	$FeCrO_4$	172
Lead Oxide	PbO	223
Lithium Oxide	Li_2O	30
Lithium Carbonate	Li_2CO_3	74
Magnesium Oxide	MgO	40
Magnesium Carbonate	$MgCO_3$	84
Manganese Oxide	MnO_2	87
Manganese Carbonate	$MnCO_3$	115
Nickel Oxide	NiO	75
Potassium Oxide	K_2O	94
Silicon Dioxide	SiO_2	60
Sodium Oxide	Na_2O	62
Strontium Oxide	SrO	103
Tin Oxide	SnO	151
Titanium Oxide	TiO_2	80
Uranium Oxide	U_3O_8	842
Vanadium Pentoxide	V_2O_5	182
Zinc Oxide	ZnO	81
Zirconium Oxide	ZrO_2	123

INDEX

ACKNOWLEDGEMENTS

Author and publishers wish to express their appreciation of the help afforded by the following in the preparation of *Practical Guide to Pottery*:

To Robert Fielden for the drawings reproduced throughout the book.

Special thanks to Michael Casson who suggested the content of the book and kindly read the manuscript, and to Milly Saunderson who typed the manuscript.

To James Peggs who kindly provided photographs of work by his students.

To Podmore & Sons, from whose fascinating catalogue is reproduced the Table of Pyrometric Cones to be found in Appendix One.

To the following books which supplied interesting source material:

Hamada Shoji, published by Asahi Shimbun Publishing Co. Quotation on page 42.
Clay and Glazes for the Potter by Daniel Rhodes, published by Pitman. Composition of earth's crust on page 11.
Pioneer Pottery, by Michael Cardew, published by Longmans. Page 7.
A Potter's Book, by Bernard Leach, published by Faber & Faber.

Illustrations

Thanks are due to the following for permission to reproduce the photographs used to illustrate this book. Credits are given spread by spread. All Victoria and Albert Museum photographs are Crown Copyright Reserved.

Cover: *Photograph by David Shapley, with thanks to Barry Guppy, The Pottery, Moreton St., London S.W.1.*

Pages
1–5   *Photographs by David Shapley, with thanks to Barry Guppy, The Pottery.*
10–11   *Plate 1: Spectrum Colour Library.*
14–15   *Pl. 2: Mary Evans Picture Library; Pl. 3: Central Press Photos.*
16–17   *Pl. 4: Mary Evans Picture Library; Pl. 5: The Fulham Pottery.*
20–21   *Pl. 6: Victoria and Albert Museum.*
22–23   *Pl. 7: Victoria and Albert Museum; Pl. 8: Victoria and Albert Museum.*
24–25   *Pl. 9: Fitzwilliam Museum.*
26–27   *Pl. 10: Thornhill School, Sunderland; Pl. 11: Author; Pl. 12: Author.*
28–29   *Pl. 13: Victoria and Albert Museum.*
30–31   *Pl. 14: Victoria and Albert Museum.*
32–33   *Pl. 15: Victoria and Albert Museum.*
34–35   *Pl. 16: Robert Fielden.*
38–39   *Pl. 17: Fitzwilliam Museum.*
42–43   *Pl. 18: Author.*
46–47   *Pl. 19–20: Lascelles Secondary School, Harrow; Pl. 21: Thornhill School, Sunderland.*
50–51   *Pl. 22: Thornhill School, Sunderland.*
58–59   *Pl. 23: Wendy and Peter Green.*
66–67   *Pl. 24: Mr & Mrs Glyn Bridges/Author.*
72–73   *Pl. 25–28: all Victoria and Albert Museum.*
74–75   *Pl. 29: Fitzwilliam Museum; Pl. 30: Fitzwilliam Museum; Pl. 31: Victoria and Albert Museum.*
76–77   *Pl. 32: Michael Casson; Pl. 33: Victoria and Albert Museum; Pl. 34: Author; Pl. 35: Fitzwilliam Museum.*
78–79   *Pl. 36: Pittrivers Museum.*
80–81   *Pl. 37: Pittrivers Museum.*
82–83   *Pl. 38: The Fulham Pottery.*
84–85   *Pl. 39: Ashmolean Museum.*
86–87   *Pl. 40–44: all Ashmolean Museum.*
88–89   *Pl. 45–46: Ashmolean Museum.*

738
GER   Gerard, Colin

Practical Guide To Pottery

53365

82-14279